Venerable Ajaan
Khao Anālayo

"The Gift of Dhamma Excels All Other Gifts"

—*The Lord Buddha*

Venerable Ajaan Khao Anālayo

A True Spiritual Warrior

Ajaan Mahā Boowa Ñāṇasampanno

Translated by Ajaan Paññāvaḍḍho

A Forest Dhamma  Publication

Venerable Ajaan Khao Anālayo

A Forest Dhamma Publication / January 2010

ISBN 974-94962-2-1
Second Printing: January 2010

Printed in Thailand by:
Silpa Siam Packaging and Printing Co., Ltd.
Tel. (662) 444-3351-9
silpa@ksc.th.com

Published by:
Forest Dhamma Books
Baan Taad Forest Monastery
Udon Thani 41000, Thailand
fdbooks@gmail.com, fdbooks@hotmail.com
www.ForestDhammaBooks.com

CONTENTS

Buddha Pūjā

Dhamma Pūjā

Sangha Pūjā

Venerable Ajaan Khao Anālayo
(1888-1983)

Relics

Bone fragments collected after the cremation of Ajaan Khao's body have transformed into countless crystal-like relics that are cherished as rare gems of purity by the Buddhist faithful.

This printing is respectfully dedicated to
Ajaan Paññāvaḍḍho, who passed away on
August 18, 2004 before his translation of Ajaan
Khao's biography could be published. May his selfless
devotion to spreading the true Dhamma be an
inspiration to all who read this book.

When Ajaan Khao lived in the forests and the mountains, he got the local villagers to lay out three different paths for walking meditation. The first path he used for paying homage to the Lord Buddha, the second for homage to the Dhamma, and the third for homage to the Sangha. He walked caṅkama on these three paths at three different times each day.

As soon as he had finished his morning meal, he began walking meditation on the Buddha Pūjā path.

Path One

Buddha Pūjā

Stepping Forth

Venerable Ajaan Khao Anālayo was born in the Year of the Rat on Sunday December 28, 1888. His natal village was Baan Bo Chaneng, located in the Nong Kaew sub-district of Amnat Charern district in the province of Ubon Ratchathani. His father's name was Phua and his mother's Rort, and their surname was Khoratha. Khao Khoratha was the fourth of seven children.

Khao Khoratha was a farmer by profession. Working hard, he prospered and made friends easily. By nature, he was honest and upright, always displaying a warm-hearted, generous attitude toward family and friends. Everyone loved and admired him. Because of this he had many acquaintances, who were all good responsible people. In contrast to nowadays when having many friends tends to lead to a lot of drinking and carousing, causing friends in this age of instant gratification to encourage each other's downfall by dragging one another headlong into a living hell, in those days people tended toward virtuous conduct, making friendships wonderfully inspiring and mutually beneficial interactions that never led to personal damage.

When he was 20 years old, his parents arranged for him to be married. His wife's name was Nang Mee. They had seven children together. He lived the life of a lay person for many years, supporting his family following the customs of the world. It seems, however, that the relationship with his wife was not a smooth and happy one, due to the fact that his wife was never content to remain faithful to her husband. She had a tendency to take advantage of his trusting nature — adulterous behaviour that became a poison damaging the heart of her partner, as well as the wealth and stability of their family. An unfaithful spouse is like a destructive parasite which so damages the relationship that husband and wife can no longer remain together.

In Ajaan Khao's case, however, one is tempted to speculate that his marital situation turned out to be a great boon for him, the fruition of some favourable *kamma*. For had he not been so emotionally traumatized, he may never have considered sacrificing everything to ordain as a Buddhist monk. In any event, it seems almost certain that he began seriously considering life as a monk because of his wife's infidelity; and that he finally decided to ordain for precisely this reason.

When a wife or a husband has a lover — or a wife has many lovers and a husband has many mistresses — the finger of blame points directly at *rāgataṅhā*, the *kilesa* of sexual craving. Never being satisfied, *rāgataṅhā* sweeps everyone into its defiling sphere of influence: *mahicchatā* — insatiable greed. To avoid damaging the lives of innocent family members, the temptation to commit adultery must be resisted at all costs. Unfortunately, this kind of behaviour is widespread and it seems to increase all the time. For as long as the people of this world are content to follow the lead of sexual craving, they will feel no inclination to view their conduct in the light of Dhamma. The Dhamma teaches: *santutthi paramaṁ dhānaṁ* — contentment is the greatest treasure. A harmonious, trusting relationship between husband and wife is the essential wealth of any family. The peace and happiness of the family depends on their being able to live in mutual trust and harmony — and on their not going the way of *mahicchatā*; that is, husbands and wives whose illicit lovers consume all their time and interest.

Rāgataṅhā, the defilement of sexual craving, is comparable to a kitchen fire — both are necessary to establishing and maintaining a successful family. Marriage is necessarily a sexual partnership, while a kitchen fire is indispensable for preparing the family's food. Just as heat and electricity are common requisites of human life, so too is *rāgataṅhā* a fundamental aspect of human relations, and the driving force behind most human behaviour. If both are used carefully, with proper circumspection, they can sufficiently fulfil people's basic needs in life. But if people carelessly fail to keep these two fires under control, they can certainly cause a conflagration that destroys everything in its path. For this reason, the wise have always taught human beings who live under the influence of the fires of greed, hatred and delusion to think in terms of Dhamma. Dhamma is like cool water that quenches fires in the heart, preventing their spreading and gaining such strength that they destroy the world we live in. So to prevent their becoming a danger to ourselves and others, we should watch over the fires of the heart in the same way that we watch over the kitchen fire to safeguard our family and our possessions.

When Ajaan Khao saw the woman he loved to the bottom of his heart change, endangering and threatening to destroy his heart in a way he never imagined possible, he made up his mind to ordain as a monk. He was disgusted and so enraged seeing his wife's blatant infidelity that he could hardly control himself. Fortunately, he had sufficient inherent virtue to realise just in time that:

"If I kill her, she will suffer enormous pain, regardless of the fact that she is guilty and knows she's guilty. After all, even an insect bite can be unbearably painful, how much more so the intense pain of death. So I must restrain myself and carefully consider the consequences before it's too late. Why am I so eager to commit such a heinous crime? It is despicable behaviour that all good people abhor and all wise men strongly denounce. What benefit can I possibly gain from killing her? All I'll gain is a heavy penalty of intense suffering bounding back to burn me. Am I the only man who has an unfaithful wife? Hasn't everyone in the world, including the Buddha, his *Arahant* disciples and respected *Ajaans,* encountered similar hellish situations in their lives? Am I really the only one? I must consider quickly and make the right decision! Otherwise, I'll so damage myself that I'll have no virtue left capable of leading me to a good rebirth in the future.

"My reaction to circumstances like this shall become the yardstick by which I measure how clever or how stupid I am, and whether I will progress successfully or whether I am doomed to failure. Throughout history, wise people have never allowed themselves to be overpowered by the evils of this world. Instead, they have thought up clever ways of turning the poisons of evil into a rich fertilizer nourishing Dhamma in the heart. So why should I be willing to render myself a worthless person by doing an evil deed just because someone else has deeply offended me? The world we live in is full of injustices — why should I allow them to dictate my behaviour? If I am unable to constrain myself now, how will I ever be able to live a life of virtue? By succumbing to the power of a sexual craving that knows no bounds, my wife has abused my trust in her. Should I now abuse her by self-righteously succumbing to the power of anger? If I take my revenge by killing both my wife and her lover, which of us would be more despicable? According to the Buddha's teaching, I would be committing such a grave *kamma* that no amount of love and compassion could absolve me or save me from a certain descent into the agonies of hell. Am I going to put my trust in the anger that is engulfing my heart at this moment, or will I put my faith in the Dhamma of the Lord Buddha — a teaching that has always effectively diminished the pain and suffering of living beings. Consider quickly and make the right decision; otherwise, the malevolent power of the *kilesas* will overtake the Dhamma and totally destroy me."

Ajaan Khao said that it was incredibly strange and amazing how at the moment that this warning thought arose, it was as if a revered *ajaan* was sitting right in front of him calming his emotions. His heart, which had been like a blazing fire ready to burn to ashes the cause of its misery, suddenly went unusually still and calm. He felt a deep sense of sadness and dismay about his wife's infidelity. At the same time, he pitied her and forgave her from the bottom of his heart. At that moment, he saw clearly the potential harm caused by anger and resentment. When Dhamma arose and his heart went completely still and quiet, Ajaan Khao felt that he had been mercifully spared from rebirth in hell. He felt relieved and supremely peaceful at that moment, as though he had been born once again within the same mind and body. This caused him to reflect back on the tight bind he had found himself in, and on how he had almost destroyed himself unwittingly by succumbing to the power of anger. He then reflected on how he should properly conduct himself so as not to become contaminated by the same kinds of evil, destructive thoughts in the future, abhorrent thoughts that appalled and disgusted him.

Previous to this incident, Ajaan Khao had thought only about how to fulfil his worldly ambitions. After his wife's infidelity inspired him to think about Dhamma, most of his thinking was focused in that direction, which in turn lead to his resolution to be ordained as a monk. He finally realised the harmfulness of the lay person's life where his hopes and dreams were more likely to meet with disappointment than they were fulfilment. In the end, he was so severely hurt that he could hardly bear it. Placing his entire faith in Dhamma, he decided to ordain and practice the way of the Buddha to the utmost of his strength and ability. Once he had informed his family and friends of his decision, he entered the local monastery as a white-robed *upāsika* with the intention of becoming a monk as soon as possible.

Ajaan Khao later explained his predicament like this: "As a lay man I worked very hard to support my family. But the fruits of my labour were just barely sufficient to meet our needs. Often we had to go without. So out of concern for my family I decided to travel to the Central Plains region and hire myself out as a farm labourer. I worked hard and saved my money; then I returned home. Unfortunately, upon my return I discovered that my wife had a lover. At that moment I nearly lost control of myself. I found them sleeping together. Having been forewarned by some of my friends in the village, I crept up on them in the middle of the night with a machete in my hand. I raised the machete over my head, ready to strike them both with all my strength. But, by chance, her lover saw me first. Trembling with fear, he raised his hands and pleaded with me to spare his life. He admitted that he had done something terribly wrong. At that very moment the thought arose: 'He's admitted his guilt. Don't do it! Don't do it! It will only make matters much worse. Nothing good can come out of it.'

"I felt pity for that man who was so terrified of dying, and my anger subsided. I quickly called the other villagers to come and bear witness so that no one would have doubt as to the truth of the situation. In front of the entire assembly, which included the village headman and all of my relatives, I pressed serious charges against my wife's lover. He responded by publicly confessing everything, and agreed to pay a fine. I then announced for all to hear that I was ceding my wife to her lover.

"Having cut off the urge for revenge, I felt relieved; although I remained deeply dismayed by what happened. I had lost faith in life, and I felt no motivation to pick up the pieces and start my worldly life over again. I thought only of how I wished to become a monk so that I could escape these circumstances and transcend this wretched world. Going beyond the world to attain *Nibbāna* following the Lord Buddha and his *Arahant* disciples was the only course I was willing to contemplate. It was for this reason that I ordained, and it is for this reason that I have practised Dhamma diligently all my life. I became a Bhikkhu in great haste because I was so disgusted and dismayed that it weighed heavily on my heart. Nothing could have stopped me at that time."

AJAAN KHAO'S ORDINATION took place at Wat Bodhi Sri monastery on May 2, 1919. Phra Khru Phuttisak was his *upajjhāya* and Ajaan Bunjan was his *kammavācariya*. He stayed at Wat Bodhi Sri studying the principles of Dhamma and *Vinaya* for six years. During his stay there, he observed that the conduct of his teachers and his fellow monks was erratic. They were often neglectful in their observance of monastic discipline and unreliable in their practice of meditation. What he saw was contrary to his own pure intentions to ordain solely for the realization of *Magga* and *Phala*. After considering the matter over and over very carefully, he decided to leave the relative security of the monastery to pursue the wandering lifestyle of a *dhutanga* monk. He then made his decision known to the abbot and his family and friends.

Entering the Dhutanga Path

Before leaving his village to practise *Kammaṭṭhāna*, Ajaan Khao received nothing but discouragement from practically everybody he met, both lay people and Bhikkhus alike. All of them said that nowadays it was impossible to attain the Path, Fruition and *Nibbāna*; that the era was long past when this could be done; that however rightly and properly one were to practise the way of the Dhamma and *Vinaya*, one would not be able to attain the desired results and reach the goal; that the practice of meditation makes people mad, so whoever wants to go mad should practise it; that if one aspires to be a good person in society, one should not drive oneself mad by going the way of *Kammaṭṭhāna*; that in this age there are no *Dhutanga Kammaṭṭhāna Bhikkhus*, except for those who sell magic yantras, mantras, lockets which have magic properties, magic potions for influencing others, ways of making people impervious to bullets and knives, knowledge of auspicious times and astrology. They assured him that as far as finding *Dhutanga Kammaṭṭhāna Bhikkhus* who actually practise the way of *Dhutanga*, there were none left nowadays. So he must not waste his time and tire himself to no purpose, for to get to a state of ease and happiness in that way was impossible.

These were some of the many obstacles which blocked the path of those who wanted to practise the way of the *Dhutangas* in those days. But Venerable Ajaan Khao was not prepared to listen to any of them, although he did not object or argue with them for it would not have been useful to either side. But deep within himself he considered that:

"These people are not the owners of the Buddhist religion, they are not the owners of the Path, Fruition and *Nibbāna*, nor have they any power to make anyone else go mad, so why should I believe what they say. I have faith only in the Lord Buddha, in the Dhamma and in the Sangha of *Sāvaka Arahants* as being truly worthy within the Triple World. Those who spoke, trying to persuade me to stop, so that I would not go the way of *Kammaṭṭhāna* and practise its various methods, are not those who are truly worthy at all. Just by looking at the behaviour and manners they display, one can know whether they are truly wise or simply foolish, and generally what their characters are like. Their objections in wanting to stop me are things which would be a waste of time for me to even consider. So I must now go away to practise the way of *Kammaṭṭhāna* as soon as I can without considering anything else. I must search for true things which accord with the basic principles of Dhamma that have been handed down to us. I must strive in this way until I reach the absolute limit of my strength and ability. If I should chance to die in the process, then I willingly give my life and entrust myself to the supreme Dhamma."

As he prepared to set out on his *dhutanga* wanderings, all his fellow Bhikkhus and many lay people gathered in the monastery to see him off. Just before he left he spoke truthfully from his heart to those who had tried to stop him so as to leave no doubt about his intentions, saying:

"When I have gone from here, unless I can teach myself to attain the ultimate level of *citta* and Dhamma I shall not return to show my face amongst you again. I am ready to die for the sake of realising the true nature of Dhamma with clarity and insight, but not for anything else. Please remember what I have said, just in case I have the right characteristics that enable me to return and meet you again. The only likelihood of my meeting you again will be if I realise the true nature of Dhamma with clarity and absolute certainty."

He said this at a time when many people were gathered there, both highly respected Bhikkhus and the lay people from his village who had faith in them as being very wise and learned monks. And all of them tried to stop him from going away. He remembered:

"At that time my heart seemed so strong it could crush a diamond to powder in an instant. It seemed as if I could leap into the sky and walk about up there for all of them to see. This was probably due to pride and high spirits in my heart — as though it were shining forth brightly for all those people to see, telling them: 'See here, the diamond radiance in this heart, can't you see it? Are you all stupid enough to disparage me, saying that I will go mad by delving into strange things? My heart is not in the same sphere as all of yours, such that you can gather it up into your clan to die worthlessly in the way a dog dies. I am not prepared to die in the way that all of you would lead me towards death right now, for I intend to die in the way that the Lord Buddha taught us — by not leaving any 'seed' of becoming remaining whatsoever. I have already died in your way so many countless times that it is impossible to tell in how many cemeteries I have ended my days. But although I may not be able to know this with my own higher knowing faculty, I have faith in the Lord Buddha and his teaching, for his higher knowing faculty was supreme and unequalled'."

As soon as he was ready, he said farewell and took his leave of all the Bhikkhus and learned people and walked away through a large crowd of lay followers. He then set out for That Phanom[1] on foot through thick forests and jungles, following paths worn by people and buffalo carts; for in those days there were no roads, not even the roughest dirt roads, but only foot paths. Many types of wild animals inhabited the forests. Large numbers of elephants and tigers roamed everywhere, since there were no villages and not as many people about as there are nowadays. Those forests were the original virgin forests, so there was a real danger that if one became lost one would have no food and might die in the forest. Often a person could walk all day without meeting anyone or seeing any sign of habitation.

Venerable Ajaan Khao walked through thick forests until he reached That Phanom. He wanted to find Venerable Ajaan

Mun and study the way of practice with him. Ajaan Khao knew of Ajaan Mun's peerless reputation and was determined to seek him out. He had heard that Ajaan Mun and Ajaan Sao were staying at Tha Bor in Nong Khai province, so from That Phanom he set out walking to Nong Khai, a distance of some 270 miles. Wandering by stages, he reached Nong Khai in several months and went to see Ajaan Mun. He related:

"I was only able to spend a short time training with him before he went away and disappeared into silence. Then I felt a sense of hopelessness for a while because I had no teacher to teach and guide me. Several years later I heard that Venerable Ajaan Mun had gone to stay and practise the way in the Chiang Mai area, so I set out to follow him by wandering in the *Dhutanga Kammaṭṭhāna* way, going along the bank of the Mekong River until I reached the province of Chiang Mai. Then I wandered about in the various districts of Chiang Mai with peace and happiness."

The places where Ajaan Khao stayed and practised were deep in the forests and hills and far away from any villages. At that time, Venerable Ajaan Mun was also wandering about in the same area, but it was not easy to find him because he always liked to wander alone away from his colleagues; and he would not readily allow others to meet him. Ajaan Khao continued following him relentlessly without success for about a year until he finally gave up hope of ever finding Ajaan Mun and began walking back toward the Northeast region. He walked as far as Lampang where he met Ajaan Waen, whom he had known previously. Ajaan Waen said that he knew where to find Ajaan Mun, so they decided to go together in search of him. They eventually found him at Wat Pa Miang Huay Sai in the Phrao district of Chiang Mai province. Ajaan Mun preferred to live alone, so Ajaan Khao and Ajaan Waen camped in the mountains nearby and came often to get instructions from him. When the *vassa* period approached, he insisted that Ajaan Khao and Ajaan Waen find another monastery to spend the retreat because the villagers supporting Ajaan Mun's retreat were poor and could not afford to support many monks.

Ajaan Khao said that he always tried to stay close by Venerable Ajaan Mun so that he could go to see him and learn from him when it was necessary. Whenever he approached Ajaan Mun to seek his advice about an aspect of Dhamma, his teacher always had compassion for him and taught him to the utmost of his ability without holding back or hiding anything — but he would never let anybody stay with him. Still, Ajaan Khao said that he was quite content that Ajaan Mun had compassion for him and taught him at those times when it was necessary to go and ask him questions. Once he had cleared up his problems, he paid his respects and left Ajaan Mun to live alone, putting into practise what he had learnt. In this manner, he travelled back and forth quite often.

After living like this for several years, Venerable Ajaan Mun very kindly let him stay with him for the *vassa* period. Ajaan Khao was so glad and so happy when Venerable Ajaan Mun told him the news that he felt as if he could float in the air, for after trying for so many years he had at last succeeded. From then on he stayed regularly with Ajaan Mun during the *vassa*. The practice and development of Ajaan Khao's *citta bhāvanā* (meditation) steadily gained strength after he went to stay in the Chiang Mai region. With a skilled teacher to guide and teach him continually, his heart seemed as though it were about to leap into the sky — so strong was his happiness and contentment in the Dhamma that arose in his heart. No longer was there any unease or sadness due to his practice being up and down — sometimes progressing and sometimes declining — as happened when he was staying in other places. From day to day his heart steadily progressed, both in *samādhi* and in wisdom, and he became engrossed in striving day and night without ever becoming satiated.

A Special Affinity for Elephants

Once Ajaan Khao was wandering *dhutanga* in the Chiang Mai mountains with Ajaan Mun and Ajaan Mahā Thong Sak. As they reached a narrow gap in the path leading up the mountain, they chanced upon a large, solitary elephant whose owner had released it and then wandered off some place. All they could see there was a gigantic elephant with huge six-foot tusks searching for food — quite a fearsome sight. They conferred among themselves about how to proceed. This was the only path up the mountain, and it allowed no room for going around the elephant. Ajaan Mun told Ajaan Khao to speak with the elephant, which was eating bamboo leaves at the side of the path. Standing about twenty yards away with its back to them, it had yet to notice their approach. Ajaan Khao addressed the elephant:

"Big brother elephant, we wish to speak with you."

At first, the elephant did not clearly hear his voice, but it did stop chewing the bamboo leaves.

"Big brother elephant, we wish to speak with you."

Clearly hearing this, the elephant suddenly swung around to face the monks. It stood stock-still, its ears fully extended.

"Big brother elephant, we wish to speak with you. You are so very big and strong. We are just a group of monks, so weak and so very frightened of you, big brother. We would like to walk past where you are standing. Would big brother please move over a bit so that we have room to pass by? If you keep standing there, it really frightens us, so we don't dare walk past."

As soon as he finished speaking, the elephant immediately turned to the side and thrust its tusks into the middle of a clump of bamboo, signalling its intention to let them pass unharmed. Seeing it facing the clump of bamboo, Ajaan Mun told the others that they could continue on as it would not bother them now. The two monks invited Ajaan Mun to walk between them, with Ajaan Khao walking in front and Ajaan Mahā Thong Sak following behind. They walked past in single file only six feet from the elephant's rear end, without incident. But as they were walking away, by chance the hook on Ajaan Mahā Thong Sak's umbrella got tangled in some bamboo just a few yards past the elephant. It defied all attempts to extricate it, so he was forced to struggle with it for quite some time. Terrified of the elephant — which was now looking right at him — he was soon drenched in sweat. Fighting desperately to disentangle the hook, he glanced up at the eyes of the elephant, which stood there like a huge stuffed animal. He could see that its eyes were bright and clear. In truth, its countenance inspired affection rather than fear, but at that moment his fear remained strong. When he finally did get free, his fear subsided, and he realised that this elephant was a very endearing animal. Seeing that they were all safely past, Ajaan Khao turned to the elephant.

"Hey, big brother, we've all passed by now. Please relax and eat in peace."

As soon as he finished speaking, the sound of crunching, breaking bamboo filled the air.

Later the monks praised this intelligent elephant, agreeing it was an animal that inspired affection and sympathy. The only faculty it lacked was the ability to speak. Ajaan Mahā Thong Sak was truly amazed how Ajaan Khao was able to speak with the elephant as though it was just another human being: 'Big brother, your little brothers are frightened and dare not pass. Please make way so that we can go by without fearing big brother.' As soon as it received that bit of flattery, it was so pleased that it immediately prepared to make way for them.

ON ANOTHER OCCASION, Venerable Ajaan Khao was spending the *vassa* period together with another Bhikkhu. Late one night when it was very quiet, he was sitting in meditation in a small hut. That night a large elephant, whose owner had let it loose to wander in the forest to find its own food, walked slowly towards the back of his hut. Ajaan Khao did not know where it had come from. Right behind his hut was a large boulder blocking the way, so the elephant could not get any closer to him. When it got to the boulder, it stretched its trunk out into the hut until it touched his klod[2] and the mosquito net above his head while he was sitting in meditation. The sound of its breathing was loud as it sniffed him, and he felt the coolness of it on his head, while his klod and mosquito net swung back and forth. Meanwhile, Ajaan Khao sat repeating the *parikamma* "Buddho", putting everything he had into it. Not having anything else to rely upon, he entrusted his heart and life to the genuine "Buddho".

The large elephant continued to stand there quietly for about two hours, as if it was waiting to catch him when he moved, ready to tear him to pieces. Once in a while he heard its breath sniffing him from outside the mosquito net. When it finally moved, it drew back, walked to the western end of his hut and reached into a basket of sour tamarinds, which lay people had brought Ajaan Khao to clean the lid of his bowl, then started to eat them, making a loud, crunching noise as if they were delicious.

Ajaan Khao thought, "Those tamarinds for cleaning my bowl lid are going to be cleaned out. Soon there will be none left for sure. If the owner of this big belly finishes them off and cannot find any more, it is sure to come into my hut and find me and tear me to bits. So I'd better go out and speak to it and tell it some things that it should know. This animal knows the language of people quite well since it has lived with people for a long time. When I speak to it, it will be more likely to listen to me than to be stubborn and difficult. If it becomes stubborn and belligerent, it will probably kill me. But even if I don't go out and talk to it, once it has eaten all the tamarinds it's bound to come this way and find me. If it is going to kill me, there will be no way to escape since it's late at night and too dark for me to see where I am going."

Having come to this decision, he left his small hut and stood in front, hiding behind a tree. He started to speak to the elephant, saying:

"Big brother, your small brother would like to say a few words to you, please listen to what I have to say to you now."

As soon as the elephant heard the sound of his voice, it went completely still and quiet without making a move. Then Ajaan Khao spoke to it in a mild, persuasive manner, saying:

"Big brother, you have been brought up by people who have looked after you at their homes until you have now become fully domesticated. You are thus fully aware of the ways of people, including the language that they speak, which they have used to teach you for many years. You know all these things very well; in fact, you know them even better than some people do. So, big brother, you should also know the customs and laws of people, and you should not just do anything that you feel like doing as it suits your fancy. When you act in ways that are contrary to the ways of human beings, you can easily upset people. Then they may harm you, or, depending on what you do, they may even kill you. People are far more intelligent than all other animals in the world. All animals fear people more than any other species. You, big brother, are in subjection to people, so you should respect their ways, for human beings are more intelligent than you are. If you're even a little bit stubborn or difficult, they beat you painfully on the head with a hook. If you are very bad, they will probably kill you.

"Please don't forget what your little brother has taught out of compassion for you. Your little brother is a Bhikkhu, so I will give you the five *sīla*. You should keep them well. Then, when you die, you will go to a state of happiness — at least you should be born as a human being with merit and the virtue of Dhamma in your heart. Should you be born higher than that, you may go to the heaven realms or *Brahmaloka* or higher still.

All of those births are far superior to being born as an animal like an elephant or a horse, which are used to draw carts or to drag logs about while being beaten with whips. Such a life is nothing but torment and trouble that lasts until one dies, without there being any chance to get free from that burden — just like the life you must put up with at present.

"Big brother, please listen carefully and make a true resolve to accept the moral precepts. They are firstly, *Pāṇātipāta*: you must not kill people or animals deliberately by taking advantage of your strength and ability to do so — and also, you must not mistreat or oppress others, whether people or animals. To do such things is to do evil. Secondly, *Adinnādāna*: you must not steal or take for yourself things which belong to others, or which others are keeping for their own use — such as the tamarinds in that basket which big brother was eating just now. They were given to me by people for cleaning the lid of my bowl. But I don't take offence at this, for I don't want you to make any evil *kamma* at all. I just mentioned it to show you that it's something that has an owner. If things such as that are not given to you, you should not eat them, nor should you walk over them, trampling on them and damaging them. Thirdly, *Kāmesu miccācāra*: you must not have sexual intercourse with any animal which already has a mate, for this is wrong. If you have sexual intercourse, it should only be with one who has no mate, for this is not wrongdoing. Fourthly, *Musāvāda*: you must not lie or deceive. Let your actions and your behaviour be true and straightforward, not deceitful in such a way that they give a wrong impression or fool others. That is also wrong and evil. Fifthly, *Surā meraya majja pamādaṭṭhāna*: you must not consume anything which causes intoxication or drunkenness, such as alcoholic liquors. To do so is wrong and evil.

"You must keep these precepts, for if you don't you can fall into hell when you die. There you will have to put up with great suffering for long periods of time — perhaps for aeons — before you reach the end of the *kamma* that led you to hell and you can rise out of it. But even after getting free from hell, there will still be some remainder of your evil *kamma* which will lead you to life after life as a ghost, a demon or an animal. In those births you will still suffer the results of the evil *kamma* you made. Only then will you be able to take birth as a human being — a birth very difficult to attain because of the bad *kamma* which oppresses you and holds you down.

"So big brother, you must remember well what I have said and practice what I have taught you. Then you will get free from life as an animal and be born as a human being or a *Devatā* in your next life for sure. That is all I have to teach you now. I hope that big brother will be glad to do these things. Now you may go find a place to rest or something to eat as you wish. Your younger brother will now go and practise his meditation. He will share some of his virtue with you and spread out *mettā* to his big brother so that you will never be lacking in happiness. Now, big brother, it is time for you to go elsewhere."

It was most remarkable that for the whole of the time that he was teaching it, that large elephant stood absolutely still, as though it were made of rock. It did not fidget or move at all, but stood motionless until he had finished speaking. Then, as soon as he had given the *sīla* with his blessings and told it to go, it began to move its huge body, making a noise like an earthquake while it drew back, turned around and went off. It walked away in a deliberate, thoughtful manner, as if it truly understood everything it had heard.

Thinking about this incident I cannot help feeling a lot of sympathy for one whose body was that of an animal, but whose heart was that of a human being, able to appreciate the teaching on good and evil that it received without being obstinate or arrogant, as one might expect from such a large and strong animal. In fact, it was very mild-mannered and appeared to appreciate the moral teaching throughout — and as soon as Ajaan Khao told it to go, it immediately turned around and went away. While listening to his teaching, it listened so attentively that it almost stopped breathing, just like those who listen to a Dhamma talk given by Bhikkhus should — with full respect for Dhamma.

Ajaan Khao was amazing as well. He was so skilled in his speech and his choice of words that even human beings would have been enraptured and carried away by his talk, much less an animal like an elephant. He used the most sweet and honeyed language with such skill that it would be rare to find anyone else who could do this, and equally rare to listen to it. So the elephant listened with rapt attention, not fidgeting or even moving its ears until he had finished giving his Dhamma talk. When he told it to go away, it obeyed and went to find something to eat in the manner of an unusually noble animal.

The whole incident makes one reflect even more deeply how if something is experienced that brings satisfaction, whether to a human or animal, that tends to make their hearing clear and lucid and their sight bright, as though night becomes day. The heart is absorbed with *pīti* — satisfaction and joyful gladness —

while listening to the enchanting words of the teaching, which are always desirable and of which one can never have enough, because they are things that are greatly valued by the heart.

Venerable Ajaan Khao continued to flatter the big elephant for quite a long time, until it became fascinated and mesmerised by the sweet, gentle words which resonated deep inside — for example:

"Big brother, you are very strong, whereas I am small and my strength cannot compare with yours — so I feel afraid of you."

Such flattery being one of the most powerful ways of enchantment, he talked like this until the great elephant went into a trance while standing there, oblivious to everything else. It would even have been glad to disgorge the sour tamarinds that it had swallowed, to put them back in the basket for its charming little brother, without keeping even the taste of them. For this act was a disgrace to the dignity of an intelligent and noble elephant — a walking store of virtue. Once its belly was full of Ajaan Khao's teachings, it went off to find food and never again came to bother him throughout the rest of the *vassa* period. It's quite remarkable that the heart of an animal can have so much understanding.

After the *vassa* Ajaan Khao left that place, wandering wherever he felt it was good to go for the purpose of practising the way of Dhamma ever higher and higher.

VENERABLE AJAAN KHAO was an earnest *Kammaṭṭhāna Bhikkhu* who possessed a resolute and courageous character — whatever he did, he did truly. When he was staying in the hills, he got the lay supporters to make up three paths for walking *caṅkama*. The first one he used for paying homage (*pūjā*) to the Lord Buddha, the second to the Dhamma and the third to the *Sāvaka Sangha* of the Lord. He walked *caṅkama* on these three paths at different times of the day according to a fixed schedule which he kept to quite strictly. As soon as he had finished his meal in the morning, he walked *caṅkama* on the first path paying homage to the Buddha, and continued walking until about midday. At two o'clock in the afternoon, he started walking on the path dedicated to the Dhamma and continued walking until 4 p.m., when it was time to sweep the grounds and bathe. When he had finished doing all his duties, he started to walk *caṅkama* on the path reserved for paying homage to the Sangha. He continued walking until 10 or 11 p.m., after which he rested, sitting in meditation for a while before lying down to sleep. As soon as he woke up he would begin his *samādhi* meditation practice again. This lasted until dawn, when he walked *caṅkama* until it was time for him to go on *piṇḍapāta*.

Some nights he would sit in meditation practice the whole night, not getting up from his seat until dawn. Normally when he sat in *samādhi* meditation, his heart was very bright after he had finished. But at those times when he sat all night in meditation, the material world disappeared entirely from his awareness, and even his physical body seemed to have gone as well. It was altogether a most remarkable and wonderful thing right from the time that he sat down to examine painful feeling (*dukkha vedanā*) until it died away and ceased due to his examination of the pain, which took his *citta* deep into a subtle and intimate state of calm. At that point, the only thing apparent to him was 'knowing', just this alone. This brought him a calm and happiness so subtle and gentle that it was quite indescribable. There were no supporting conditions *(ārammaṇa)*, however subtle, present in the *citta*. This means that the elements of existence *(loka dhātu)* disappeared simultaneously with the disappearance of the supporting conditions. This state remained until the *citta* withdrew from it, after which the supporting conditions that are the usual companions of the *citta* gradually returned, bit by bit. Afterwards he would continue working at his practice in the normal way.

When the *citta* has integrated and gone down into a state of calm, it may remain in that state for several hours, but there is no feeling of it being a long time such as it might normally appear to be. This must surely be the state of *eka citta, eka dhamma* [3] just within the heart alone, without there being anything else to form a duality. Only when withdrawing from that state is it possible to know that the *citta* integrated into a state of calm and remained there for so long, for so many hours. On those nights when his meditation practice went smoothly and attained calm easily, even if he sat the whole night through, it seemed like he had only been sitting for two or three hours. There were simply no hindrances to oppress him.

VENERABLE AJAAN KHAO tended to encounter dangerous situations in connection with elephants more than any other animals. Soon after the previous encounter, he met another large elephant in the Mae Pang district of Lampang Province — and this time he was almost unable to save himself. This one was a truly wild, forest elephant and not one that had lived with and been looked after by people, like the previous ones.

It was at night and Ajaan Khao was walking *caṅkama* when he heard the sound of an elephant crashing through the jungle breaking branches and making a lot of noise. It was rushing towards him, getting closer every minute, and there was no time for him to run away from it. Then he remembered how forest elephants are usually afraid of fire. So he quickly left the *caṅkama* path and went to get all his remaining candles from the place where he was staying. He then stuck them into the ground all along the sides of his *caṅkama* path and lit them as fast as he could. To any person who saw it, this would be a beautiful, peaceful sight, but it is hard to say how an elephant will react to it. By the time he had finished setting up the candles, the elephant was almost upon him, giving him no possible way of escape. All he could do was to set up a 'true resolve' (*sacca adhiṭṭhāna*) that the supernatural power of the Lord Buddha, the Dhamma and the Sangha might come to help and protect him, a servant of the Lord Buddha, against this huge elephant. By that time the elephant had arrived. Stopping about two meters away from him at one side of his *caṅkama* path, it stood there without moving, its ears spread out. It was clearly visible in the candle light, its huge body appearing as large as a hill.

Meanwhile, Ajaan Khao started walking *caṅkama*, pacing back and forth as if he was not concerned about the elephant at all – although in fact he was so afraid of it that he could hardly breathe. When he first saw it charging towards him, so strong and aggressive, he focused his attention solely on "Buddho" and held on to it tenaciously as the guarantor of his safety. Apart from that, he thought of nothing else. He did not even let his thoughts go out to the giant elephant as large as a hill which had come to stand by the side of his *caṅkama* path, for he was afraid that his *citta* might slip from "Buddho", which was his best refuge at that time. "Buddho" and the *citta* then became one and the same thing until the heart lost all fear and there remained just 'knowing' and the repetition of "Buddho" which were blended into one.

Meanwhile, the elephant just stood there like a mountain, looking at him without fidgeting or moving, its ears spread wide as if to indicate that it was not ready to accept any friendly advances. This accorded with the manner in which it charged towards Ajaan Khao when it first approached him, coming straight for him without hesitating. It acted as though it intended to crush him to death — but when it reached him it just stood there like a lifeless dummy.

As soon as the *citta* and "Buddho" went inward and came together, becoming one and the same thing, Ajaan Khao lost all fear. In fact, he felt positively bold and daring, confident that he could have walked right up to the elephant without the least feeling of fear. Having thought about it, he realised that to walk right up to such a wild jungle animal would be an act of carelessness based on conceit, which he shouldn't do. So he kept on fearlessly walking *cankama* in competition with the standing elephant, as though nothing could happen that would be any danger to him.

The elephant must have stood there for about an hour, by which time the candles were almost finished. Some had already gone out and the rest would not last much longer when the elephant backed away, turned round and walked off by the way it had come. It then went looking for food in the forest around that area, where it could be heard breaking branches and treading on dead wood, making a lot of noise.

This was the first time that Venerable Ajaan Khao saw for himself the extraordinary power of the *citta* and "Buddho". He was faced with a critical situation without any way to escape or hide, so there was no alternative but to face up to it using these methods — if he died it would be only because there was no way to avoid it. This experience made him fully confident that no matter what happened, if the *citta* and "Buddho" became intimately blended together in a natural way, nothing could possibly do any harm to him. He said that he became absolutely convinced of this and has remained so ever since.

It was also very strange how the elephant, instead of becoming wild and violent when it reached him, just stood there quite calmly, its ears spread wide as it watched him walking in meditation without getting tired of it. Once it had seen enough, it drew back, turned round and went on its way searching for food in a manner that showed its stomach had lost all its former aggression.

One cannot help but feel more sympathy for this elephant than for the previous one, which was a domesticated animal that knew the language of people quite well. But this elephant had been a wild animal living in the forest since birth — and it must have been over a hundred years old by then. As it was most unlikely that this one knew the language of people, Ajaan Khao did not speak to it at all. Instead, he simply continued walking *caṅkama*. Unlike the first elephant, this one did not have a halter around its neck. The villagers later told him that it was a wild elephant that had been the leader of a herd for a long time. Why it should have been wandering about on its own at that time nobody could say — perhaps it just left the herd for a short time.

Even after the elephant had gone, Ajaan Khao continued walking *cankama* with an amazing feeling in his heart as he realised the value of that elephant, which had come to help his *citta* to see the wonderful nature of Dhamma in connection with fear and fearlessness. It enabled him to understand it with absolute clarity, leaving no room for any doubt at all. For that reason, it would not be wrong to look on this elephant as being something created by the *Devas* for his benefit. Normally, forest elephants are not used to people, nor do they act peacefully towards them. Only when they are truly overpowered and cannot attack do they quickly flee and try to escape to save themselves.

"But this one came walking straight towards me of its own free will. With its eyes wide open, it came right up close, well within the light of the candles that I had set in place. But it did not squash me or tear me to pieces; nor was it startled and frightened by the fire of the candles, for it did not run away into the forest to save itself from the fire. Instead, after walking up to me in a bold, imposing manner, like it was the 'boss', it just stood there for over an hour, appearing neither aggressive nor afraid. After that, it simply went away. This is what made me think about that animal with amazement, so much so that I have not forgotten it to this day.

"Because my heart had full faith in Dhamma from then on, no matter where I wandered or where I lived, I was never afraid. As it says in the *Dhammapāda*: 'Dhamma guards those who practise the way' — Dhamma never lets them die, buried in mud or water like an old log of wood.

"Knowledge of the *citta* and Dhamma that truly reaches the heart is most likely to be found at those times when we are in a critical situation. When a situation is not really critical, the *citta* tends to act up and become agitated by endless kinds of *kilesas* – so much so that we can hardly keep up with them. In fact, we are likely to let them inundate us even though we see them in full view. It's as if we are unable to restrain the *kilesas*, or even keep pace with them long enough to deal with them effectively. But when the situation is truly critical so that we are actually driven into a corner, the *citta* and Dhamma become strengthened – though where the strength comes from is hard to say. The heart then bows down and submits, putting its faith in Dhamma without resisting. Then, when we decide to focus it on any aspect of Dhamma, it stays right there without balking. This is probably due to the fear of dying, which might well happen if the *citta* were uncooperative. So the *citta* becomes compliant and 'easy to teach', thus losing its stubbornness at such times.

"This is probably the reason why *Dhutanga Kammaṭṭhāna Bhikkhus* like going into the forests and hills; even though they are quite afraid of death, and one part of their hearts does not want to go to such places. My *citta* was like that. I cannot speak for other people's hearts, but if they are determined and fully committed to training themselves so as to get to the causes and reach the results of the way of truth, it should be much the same for them as well. The *citta* is the dwelling place of both Dhamma and the *kilesas*, factors that can make people feel either full of courage or full of fear, full of goodness or full of evil. Training in accordance with the right causes brings those results which are the purpose and aim of Dhamma. Such training is able to make all the various kinds of *kilesas* surrender and vanish until they have all gone without leaving any trace or seed that could grow again.

"For myself, I have a rather coarse and rough character, so I tend to have confidence in the strict discipline and rough methods that enable me to counteract those gross natural tendencies within me called the *kilesas*. Like that time when the large elephant came walking up to me while I was walking *caṅkama*. That was a time when I clearly saw the *kilesas* as well as the Dhamma of the Lord Buddha within my heart. Normally, the heart which is dominated by the *kilesas* is very difficult to discipline and train. Sometimes, those who set out to destroy their *kilesas* end up dying before they succeed in doing so. That is because of the mean tenacity of the *āsavas*[4] which have been feeding on our hearts for many ages. But as soon as I got to the point where there was no escape — when that great elephant came to help me — the most stubborn *kilesas*, the ones which had been so clever at resisting my efforts, all went into hiding — though where they went I don't know. Then it became easy to instruct the heart. When I ordered the heart to remain fixed to an aspect of Dhamma, it immediately agreed and did so. It was as if oil had been put in the machinery so that there was virtually no friction as there had been before.

"As soon as the *kilesas* left the heart, the Dhamma, which was already developed and just waiting there, arose at the same moment and shone forth brightly. Simultaneously, courage and fearlessness towards everything immediately arose within the heart. All those things that I had sought for so long were there for me to see and admire to my hearts content. Meanwhile, the fear of death had disappeared — where to I don't know, but it enabled me to see quite clearly that fear is a *kilesa* which has always asserted control over my heart. As soon as the fear that was oppressing and deceiving my heart disappeared — even though it may not have disappeared entirely — I saw quite clearly at that moment how baneful a thing it is. After that, whenever fear arose, as it did at times, I knew that what I experienced then was enough to remind me that: 'This fear is not my friend, but an enemy who has come in the guise of a friend.' It could no longer make my heart have confidence in it as before. I resolved that throughout my life of striving for Dhamma I will endeavour to drive it out every time it arises, until the essential nature of this enemy posing as a friend has entirely disappeared from my heart. Only then can I relax and be happy and free of all kinds of concerns and anxieties.

"It seems to me that if we take refuge in Dhamma, take real interest in Dhamma, love and attend closely to Dhamma and practise it truly in the way that the Buddha proclaimed it to us with complete certainty and true *mettā*, then the realisation of Dhamma at its various levels will no longer be beyond our reach. Certainly we will be able to experience Dhamma naturally, in the same way that they realised it at the time of the Lord Buddha.

"The reason why the present age and its people are so different from those at the time of the Lord Buddha, in so far as the ways of the path and its fruition are concerned, is that we ourselves act in ways that oppose our own development by merely wanting results without being interested in their causes, that is, whether we are practising rightly or wrongly. In truth, we should be adjusting and altering our actions of body, speech and mind to make them conform to Dhamma — which is the way of action leading to the Path, Fruition and *Nibbāna*. If we constantly examine and test ourselves against the standard of Dhamma for the purpose of attaining whatever we have set our hearts on, we will at least succeed in attaining that purpose to our satisfaction, so long as our mindfulness and wisdom are strong enough. Whether in the time of the Lord Buddha or in our present age, the *kilesas* must be corrected and got rid of by means of Dhamma. It's comparable to diseases that have been prevalent in all ages — they can all be cured by using the right remedy. I have had faith in this for a long time, and the longer I go on practising, the deeper it becomes buried in my heart, until nothing can remove it."

Ajaan Mun's Ascetic Path

Ajaan Khao always vividly remembered the words that Venerable Ajaan Mun spoke when they stayed together, for they had penetrated deep into his heart. His unshakeable faith in Ajaan Mun grew deeper and deeper until it became one with his heart. Ajaan Mun taught him the true way of practice in this way:

"When watching the *kilesas* and searching for Dhamma, no one should overlook the heart, which is the place where the *kilesas* and Dhamma all dwell. Both the *kilesas* and Dhamma are to be found only in the heart and not elsewhere in any time or place whatsoever. They arise in the heart, develop in the heart and die away in the heart — which is the one who knows them. Trying to cure the *kilesas* or search for Dhamma in other places is useless. Even if you were to spend the rest of your life doing so, you would never come across them as they truly are. Even after dying and being reborn many times, you would still come across only *kilesas* that have arisen from the heart, and experience the discontent and suffering that comes from them. By searching for Dhamma in the heart, you will gradually start to find it. It will then increase steadily, depending on the intensity with which you strive for it. Time and place are merely conditions which can promote or suppress the *kilesas* and Dhamma, causing them to develop or deteriorate accordingly.

"Thus, for instance, forms and sounds are conditions which promote the *kilesas* that are already in the heart, causing them to develop and increase. On the other hand, going to practise meditation in the hills and forests is done for the purpose of promoting the Dhamma that dwells in the heart, causing it to greatly increase.

"The real *kilesas* and Dhamma are within the heart, whereas the conditions that increase or suppress them are to be found everywhere, both internally and externally. That is why the *ajaans* teach their followers to avoid enticing things which are disturbing to the heart, things that tend to make those *kilesas* within their hearts become more audacious — such as the many things experienced through the senses. In addition, they also teach their followers to wander in mountains and forests so they can live in peaceful solitude. There they can much more easily practise the way and so gradually eliminate their *kilesas*, thus diminishing the round of birth and death (*vaṭṭa*) within their hearts by using these methods.

"For this reason, finding a suitable place for the purpose of striving to practise the way is very important — it is the right method for one who is ordained and hopes to attain freedom from *dukkha* in his heart. This follows the basic principles of the Dhamma that the Lord Buddha formulated for his followers after he saw clearly for himself what things were dangers to their purpose. By staying at times in ordinary places and at other times in unusual and lonely places, your attitude towards the place where you are staying is always changing, so you don't become too complacent. But when you stay a long time in one place, the *citta* becomes overly familiar with that place. Those who are reflective and watchful of themselves will know immediately when this happens, so they will quickly change and move to another place so as to find the right conditions to prevent themselves from relaxing to the point of carelessness. Complacency gives the *kilesas* an opportunity to muster their strength and thus bring about your ruin without you being aware of what is happening. But when you correct the situation right away, without being careless or indifferent to it, the *kilesas* are not likely to have any chance to build up enough strength to ruin the *citta* and the Dhamma within it. You are then able to move forward without deteriorating.

"Those who train themselves to recognize what is dangerous must have mindfulness continually present in the heart, reflecting and knowing in the present without slipping away into forgetful indulgence. By not slipping into forgetful indulgence, you create a protective barrier against many kinds of *kilesas* which have not yet arisen, thus giving them no opportunity to arise. As for the *kilesas* that are still there — those that have yet to be entirely cured — it prevents them from becoming more troublesome and arrogant. It also encourages you to get rid of them using unrelenting mindfulness, wisdom, faith and effort.

"If your mindfulness is strong, then any place which instils fear in the *citta* becomes a charnel ground for the cremation of all the *kilesas* by means of the ascetic Dhamma[5], that is, effort that has mindfulness and wisdom as the means of burning the *kilesas* to destruction. The *jhānas*, *samādhi*, *paññā* (wisdom) and *vimutti* (liberation), will all be absolutely clear to the heart in that place where you practise in the right way. Whether it's the *kilesas* losing their power, or the *kilesas* dying away steadily, or the *kilesas* being entirely eliminated, it will happen in the heart, aided by a place which is well suited to someone who strives with zeal in everything in all ways. Other than the heart, there is no other place where all the *kilesas* arise and cease. This one must keep in mind and take to heart: *The place where Dhamma thrives is where the kilesas will decline and die away entirely. What we call 'the place', those who practise the way should always know, is in the 'heart' alone and nowhere else.*

"Therefore, you should struggle to cut the *kilesas* to pieces and destroy them without fear or favour on the battlefield — which is the heart — while depending on a suitable environment as a supporting condition to enable you to be victorious, to gain salvation and to reach the highest point of human attainment by the persistence of your own striving. You must not go astray and be uncertain of the way, thinking that the *kilesas* and the great mass of your own *dukkha* are to be found anywhere else but within the sphere of the heart.

"From the first beginnings my own practice — which was rather haphazard because I had no teacher who could teach and train me properly — until I became a teacher myself with my own followers, I have never seen this mass of *dukkha* any-where but in the heart. Nor have I ever seen any unimaginably strange or truly wonderful things in any other place except the heart, which is the abode of Dhamma, and all the *kilesas* as well. *It is Dukkha and Samudaya, which also exist in the heart of each one of us, that exercise such great power over everything in the three worlds. For they are able to completely block the way which leads to the Path, Fruition and Nibbāna.* Considering the means, or 'tools', for digging out and clearing away *dukkha* and its cause so that the Path, Fruition and *Nibbāna* may be clearly revealed, nothing in the three worlds is able to accomplish this better than *Nirodha* and *Magga*[6], which also exist within the same heart. Just these Four Noble Truths tell the whole story.

"You must not long for other times, places or people, for this is a danger that wastes a lot of time and slows your devel-opment without being of any value at all. Thinking like this, rather than thinking about the *kilesas* and Dhamma within your heart, contradicts the purpose and aim of the Great Teacher — the Lord Buddha — who bestowed his Dhamma teaching on the world — a teaching which is correct and suit-able in all respects at all times."

That, in essence, was the teaching which Venerable Ajaan Mun taught Ajaan Khao in a fully reasoned way while was living with him in Chiang Mai province. Ajaan Khao always remembered it quite clearly, for it was buried in his heart with no room for doubt.

Sometimes Ajaan Khao had questions which, when he asked them, Ajaan Mun would admonish him for casually asking questions without having first considered the principles of Dhamma to see in which direction the truth lies. One such question he asked was:

"At the time of the Lord Buddha, according to his biography and other writings, large numbers of people attained the Path, Fruition and *Nibbāna*, and quickly as well. Far more people attained then than nowadays, for few people manage to get there now. Also, those who do attain nowadays seem to do so much slower."

Venerable Ajaan Mun immediately asked him: "How do you know that there are hardly any who attain the Path, Fruition and *Nibbāna* nowadays, and that those who do, do so much more slowly?"

Ajaan Khao replied: "Well, I have never heard of people attaining *Nibbāna* like they used to in those days. According to what is written in the old books, many attained *Nibbāna* simultaneously each time the Lord Buddha gave them a talk on Dhamma, and many others did so soon afterward when they went out to practise the way on their own. It seems that they attained very quickly and easily, making it a joy to read about their attainments. But nowadays, people strive until they almost die without seeing the type of results which one feels should come from such effort — which causes those who practise to become discouraged and undermines their efforts."

Venerable Ajaan Mun then asked him: "In the old books, does it say that all those who practised the way in those days attained quickly and easily? Or were there also those who practised the way with difficulty, some of them gaining understanding slowly and some quickly, as well as those who practised the way easily, some gaining understanding slowly and some quickly? Such things depend on people's inherent levels of understanding and their basic temperaments, which vary greatly with different types of people."

Ajaan Khao answered, saying: "Yes, they did vary quite considerably, and they certainly did not all attain quickly and easily. There were those who practised with difficulty, some of whom attained slowly and some quickly. But I still feel that it was very different from the situation nowadays, even though people differed in the same way then as they do now."

Venerable Ajaan Mun then explained: "This difference comes from the teachers and how correctly and precisely they can lead the way. There is also a great discrepancy between the power of the virtuous characteristics (*vāsanā*) of the Lord Buddha and the *Sāvakas* who followed the Buddha and that of people today — the difference is almost beyond comparison. In addition, the interest that people have in Dhamma nowadays is so different from the time of the Lord Buddha. Even the characteristics of people that are derived from their background in this life are very different today from what they were back then. So when there are all these differences, it's hardly possible that the results will be the same.

"But there is no need for us to talk about other people of other ages, which would take a very long time and be tiresome. In ourselves we display a coarseness that disturbs us all the time, even though we are ordained monks who believe that we strive diligently when we walk *caṅkama* and sit in *samādhi bhāvanā*. These, though, are just bodily activities. The heart, on the other hand, is not striving in any way that corresponds to these activities at all. All it does is think in ways that accumulate the *kilesas* and cause disturbance, while all along we believe that we are striving by means of these activities. When this is the case, the result is bound to disturb and trouble the heart regardless of when or where we are. Thus we conclude that, although striving to our utmost, we have not gained the results which we should have. But, in fact, while walking *caṅkama* and sitting in *samādhi* we have been accumulating harmful poisons without our being in the least aware of it. This is how we fail to strive truly and properly as it should be done.

"So, there is really no comparison between the time of the Lord Buddha — when their striving was genuine and truly concerned with gaining freedom from *dukkha* — and this present age when we merely play, like children with their toys. In fact, the more we try to make comparisons, the more we show off our *kilesas* and our incompetence. For myself, even though I live in this age of insincerity and deceit, I do not agree with you criticising the Buddhist religion, and yourself, as you did just now. If you still see that you have some virtue and truth left within you, you should try to act in accordance with the plan of action that the Lord Buddha taught so rightly. Avoid the plan of action of the *kilesas* that leads you along their way in everything you do, all the time — even while you believe that you are actually striving in the way of Dhamma. The Path, Fruition and *Nibbāna* are universal treasures that the Lord Buddha said may be acquired by anybody. They are treasures that you will realise to your complete satisfaction one day for sure, so long as you do not keep thinking how difficult it is and how slow your attainment comes — which are nothing but obstacles in your way.

"When we practise by striving like someone who feels, due to a weak, half-hearted resolve, that his body will break apart if he continues, we are like lazy inconsequential fools who think they can bore a hole through a mountain using a small auger — and they are very anxious to do this within the time of a single day. It is so ludicrous that those who really do strive with sharp wisdom just laugh at it. We should consider the manner of striving of those who were Sons of the *Sākya* — the *Sāvaka* disciples of the Buddha himself — to see how they acted. Then compare that with our own striving, which is like someone going to the shore just to smack the sea with his hand — it's enough to make one disheartened seeing that his desire for *Nibbāna* extends only to getting his hands wet! Think about how the *kilesas* are like an ocean and the efforts we make are like the water on our hands — how far apart are they? People in this age of just 'wetting their hands in the ocean' make little in the way of effort, yet their intention is to get free from the realm of *saṁsāra*. When this does not happen as they expect it to, they find some excuse to blame the religion, or the time, or the place and the people of this or that age. They are not in the least ashamed of the way they display their own incompetence and stupidity, which causes those *ajaans* who are truly wise and skilled to feel disheartened and to laugh wryly, saying that there is no way in which they can do anything about such people.

"To invest only a small amount of capital in a useless manner, and then to expect the most enormous returns on one's investment, is the way of an incompetent fool who builds his own charnel ground for cremating himself and remains engulfed in the flaming mass of his own *dukkha*. The round of *saṁsāra* never weakens its hold on him, so he never has a chance to get free from it.

"The question that you asked me — which was in effect praising the teaching of Buddhism and praising the age, the place and the people at the time of the Lord Buddha, while at the same time criticising the teaching, the age, the place and people nowadays — were the words of praise and blame of an incompetent fool who puts obstructions in his own path until he cannot find a way to crawl out to safety. It was the question of someone who is incompetent, the question of someone who puts thorns in his own path to obstruct himself. It was not a question designed to clear the way of obstacles so that you can move forward confidently with an interest in freeing yourself from the *kilesas* by means of the *Svākkhāta* Dhamma — the well-taught Dhamma — which is the 'middle way' that was given impartially to all those beings in the world who have enough interest to practise the way rightly. If you only had the mindfulness and wisdom to shed all these things from yourself, you would be worthy of some admiration.

"It's like various kinds of diseases which people get: if people take the right remedy to make them feel better, then the cure is likely to be effective. But if they are not interested in looking after themselves and treating the disease, it will probably get worse and could even become dangerous — except for minor complaints such as the common cold or minor skin troubles that cure themselves without special attention.

"The '*kilesa*' diseases, which are not in the class of self-healing minor ailments, must be treated with the right medicine. That medicine is the Dhamma-way of striving following the pattern which the Sons of the *Sākya* practised. You can be fully confident that this remedy will quell and get rid of all the *kilesas*, however strong they may be. If you were to think in this way, I could feel more at ease about you. I could admire you as someone who shows cleverness in his thinking; as someone who has confidence in his own ability to pass beyond the realm of *saṁsāra*; as someone who has faith in the ability of the Lord Buddha and his religious Teaching, faith that he penetrated Dhamma with his intuitive ability and then spread it abroad as the *Sāsana dhamma* in a proper manner. For his Teaching was a 'Dhamma of Salvation' *(Niyyānika dhamma)*, truly able to lead beings to freedom.

"So don't blame and criticise yourself, saying that your *kilesas* are so thick that you can only learn Dhamma slowly, while at the same time having no interest in curing them. Don't blame the Lord Buddha, saying that he did not formulate and teach Dhamma in a way that was equally suitable for his own time and for all other ages. Don't blame the Dhamma, saying that it is incapable, or not penetrating enough, to cure the *kilesas* of beings in this modern age in the way it did at the time of the Lord Buddha.

"I am not denying the fact that the strength of people's *kilesas* is different from what it used to be, and I agree that people at the time of the Lord Buddha had far less of them than people do nowadays. The mode of teaching was also very different from what it is today, as were the teachers, who were mostly 'seers' with great understanding and true seeing. The Great Teacher was the Leader of the *Sāvakas* in formulating and teaching Dhamma to his followers and others. Therefore, the teaching was never wrong and never deviated from the truth, for it came straight from the heart of the Lord and from the hearts of his followers, which were completely purified. From this purity of heart they proclaimed the Dhamma, teaching others in language that was fresh and direct without anything hidden or anything mixed in that was wrong or distorted.

"Those who listened to this Dhamma were intent on the truth. They fully committed themselves to it. So the situation was entirely suitable for both teacher and pupil. And so the results came stage by stage. Being self-evident, they fulfilled the expectations of those people who were looking for truth. Because of that, they encountered no problems which could interfere with their development. It was for this reason that in those days many people attained *Magga* and *Phala* each time the Great Teacher or his *Sāvaka* disciples gave Dhamma teachings — whereas nowadays hardly anybody can attain. It's as though somehow people are no longer people and Dhamma is no longer Dhamma, so no results come from the practice. But in fact, people are people and Dhamma is Dhamma, as they always were. But people are not interested in Dhamma now, so the Dhamma that enters them does not reach the heart. As a result, people remain just people and Dhamma remains just Dhamma, which is not likely to be of much use in bringing about the final attainment. Even if a large number of people listened to an exposition of the whole *Ti-piṭaka,* it would be merely like pouring water on a dog's back — the dog immediately shakes it all off until there is none left. In a similar way, the Dhamma has no meaning in the hearts of people, much as water is of no consequence on the back of a dog."

Venerable Ajaan Mun then asked Ajaan Khao: "When you asked that question just now, was your heart like a dog's back? Or what was it like that you blindly placed blame only on the Dhamma, saying that it had not brought you the results of the Path, Fruition and *Nibbāna* the same easy way it did in the time of the Lord Buddha. Why don't you think about your own heart, which is shaking off the Dhamma from itself faster than a dog can shake water off its back? If you'll only reflect back and consider your own faults and failings, some Dhamma may find a place to seep into your heart and remain there. Then it won't simply flow through it like water flowing down a channel without any reservoir to store it — which is how you are at present.

"The nature of people's *kilesas* at the time of the Lord Buddha was a matter of their own virtue and merit, a fact which should not affect us or make difficulties for us nowadays. People today have their own *kilesas* of various kinds which create trouble for them until there is hardly anywhere in the world where they can live normally. If people don't have enough interest in curing their *kilesas* so that they gain some freedom from the 'fire' with which they 'burn' each other by always criticizing one another, then it won't matter at all what age they live in. The same holds true for those who have no interest in directing their criticisms towards themselves — towards the one who is creating the 'fire' to 'burn' himself and cause all sorts of trouble to others now — in the present. Turning criticism towards yourself is a way of exorcising the fires of lust, hate and delusion — at least to the extent of finding a way to gain some degree of calm and happiness, so that you are not roasted by these fires beyond your endurance. This is the way it should be with human beings, who are far more clever than any other species in the world."

Ajaan Khao later explained the affect that Venerable Ajaan Mun's forceful admonitions had on him:

"Venerable Ajaan Mun used to scold me quite fiercely for asking questions which had no practical solution, although I didn't ask such questions very often. But when Venerable Ajaan Mun responded to these questions by treating them as if they were thorns and splinters obstructing the *Sāsana*, I felt that it forced me to see my own faults. I would feel uneasy about it for many days, even though I actually had no doubt that people nowadays could practise Dhamma. But Ajaan Mun would still scold me, 'shredding' me with his fierce language, which I reckon was right and suitable for someone like me who was always talking and so couldn't be quiet and contented. On the other hand, it was also quite beneficial because I was able to hear a Dhamma teaching that went straight to my heart.

"Actually, what I have just told you is no more than a fraction of the deep, spirited and fiery Dhamma which he delivered; for his Dhamma was deeper than the ocean and more fiery than the fires of hell. He also brought up the questions I had asked him in the past to stir me up time after time. Sometimes he did this right in the middle of a meeting when all the other Bhikkhus were gathered there to hear him speak. He would reveal my evil ways, talking about my wrong views *(micchādiṭṭhi)* and likening me to a *Devadatta* destroying the *Sāsana*. He would tear me into pieces, until there was nothing good left, going on like that for a long time without letting up, until some of the other Bhikkhus began to wonder about it. Afterwards, they would come to ask me whether what Ajaan Mun said was true. I had to explain how the questions I asked were not a true indication of my attitude, but that it was just a method of getting him to speak about Dhamma. Normally, if nobody asked him strange and unusual questions, he did not speak Dhamma like that. But I suppose I was rather stupid in my choice of questions, for I jumped in with both feet and gave him the hammer to hit me. Maybe I should have asked more normal and less inflammatory questions so that I could listen to Dhamma that was more sweet and soothing."

Generally speaking, it was as Ajaan Khao said: when Venerable Ajaan Mun was asked questions that were not in any way strange or unusual, he simply answered in a normal way. Even though it was still Dhamma, his way of speaking was smooth and normal so it made no lasting impression on one's heart. But when asked a strange, unusual question, he became quite animated, and the import of the Dhamma which he brought forth was truly satisfying — as was already described in the "Biography of Venerable Ajaan Mun".

In truth, Ajaan Mun had no doubts about Ajaan Khao's views, although the way he scolded him made it appear as though he was doubtful. It was merely the way of a skilled *ajaan* teaching Dhamma. He often changed his attitude and his style of teaching in order to arouse those who were listening, making them ponder his teachings in a way that they would remember for a long time. Otherwise, they might remain complacent, clinging to their own stupidity with no interest in thinking about anything — like a frog sitting and looking at a lotus flower without any purpose. But as soon as Ajaan Mun 'rapped them on the head with his knuckles', it was as though their ears and eyes became brighter. Those *Dhutanga Kammaṭṭhāna Bhikkhus* who followed Venerable Ajaan Mun liked being stirred up and rapped on the head frequently to hold their attention and make them think.

When he simply talked in a smooth and even manner, they would listen quiescently, there being nothing to arouse and catch the heart to make it excited, concerned and a bit frightened. Their hearts then tended to go to sleep internally when there was no method capable of making their minds active and thoughtful. Then those *kilesas* that were waiting to take over were likely to find an opportunity to escape and go about distracting their attention and causing trouble, because the method of teaching was not equal to the ability of the *kilesas*.

But when they received an unusual form of teaching from Venerable Ajaan Mun — as when he was asked a question that warranted such a way of teaching — their mindfulness and wisdom were stirred up and became brighter and sharper. So, although Ajaan Khao was partly right and partly wrong in asking Venerable Ajaan Mun questions, they were Dhamma questions from which he could expect to gain a lot of value in the same way he had often done in the past.

Dhamma Principles in the Heart

The first year that Ajaan Khao spent the *vassa* period with Venerable Ajaan Mun in the Chiang Mai region, an indescribable enthusiasm and joy arose in his heart. This opportunity was a just reward for the several years he had followed Ajaan Mun, when he had heard his teaching at times in various places but was only allowed to stay with him for brief periods, which was not truly satisfying. During those early years he would be driven away by Ajaan Mun after a short time, and told he must live in a separate location. Finally he was fortunate enough to have Ajaan Mun give him the opportunity to join him for a *vassa* period. This made him so happy that he increased his striving greatly until he was hardly taking any sleep at all – sometimes spending the whole night striving at his meditation practice. Then one night his *citta* became fully integrated, dropping down into a state of calm where it had a complete rest for some time before withdrawing to normal consciousness. He was filled with wonder at the brightness of his heart, which went beyond anything he had ever experienced before. It caused him to become completely absorbed in Dhamma until the light of dawn appeared. That night he did not sleep at all. In the morning he got up at the usual time and went about his duties, helping to clean and arrange things at Ajaan Mun's hut and taking his bowl, robes and other things to the place where he ate food in the *sālā*.

When Ajaan Mun came from the place where he did his meditation practice, it seemed that he watched Ajaan Khao unusually closely. Ajaan Khao himself noticed this and felt very self-conscious, afraid that he may have done something wrong. After a short while Venerable Ajaan asked him:

"How is your meditation practice going now? Last night your *citta* was much brighter than it has been at any time since you came to stay with me. This is how you must do it! This is the right way for one who searches for Dhamma. Do you understand where Dhamma is now? Last night, where was that brightness?"

He answered: "The brightness was in my heart, sir". But he felt afraid and embarrassed until he almost started shivering, for he had never before been praised and asked a question at the same time like this. Venerable Ajaan Mun then asked him:

"Where was the Dhamma before this that you could not see it? You have now seen Dhamma. From now on, you must always know that Dhamma is in the heart. In the future you must maintain well the level of your *citta* and the level of your efforts in meditation. You must not let them deteriorate. This is the ground[7] of the *citta*, the ground of the Dhamma, the ground of your faith in Dhamma and the ground of the Path, Fruition and *Nibbāna* – all of them are just there. You must be confident and resolute in your striving if you want to transcend *dukkha*. You have got to make the effort just there, in the heart. You can be absolutely certain that nowhere else but just this one place you can get free from *dukkha*.

"You must not grope around blindly in your practice, for you are no longer blind so there is no need to do so. Last night I sent the flow of my *citta* out to look at you and I saw your *citta* brightly illuminating everything around you. Throughout the night, every time I sent my *citta* out to look it was the same way. I did not get any sleep last night either. Part of the time I spent in *samādhi bhāvanā*, part of the time I was receiving *Deva* guests and part of the time I was sending out my *citta* to see how you were getting on. It went on like this until dawn without having any sense of time. As soon as I came out of *bhāvanā* I had to ask you about it, because I have always wanted to know about my fellows in Dhamma. Was it peaceful, was it blissful that time?"

Not daring to answer Ajaan Mun, Ajaan Khao remained silent. He felt that Ajaan Mun had already looked right through him and could see his lungs and liver and everything else, so what would be the use of telling him? From then on he was much more afraid of Ajaan Mun, and much more careful where he was concerned. Even prior to that, he was quite sure that Ajaan Mun could know the minds and hearts of people as he wished. But that day he experienced it for himself, which made him that much more certain. So he became very afraid of him in a way that's hard to describe.

From that day on, he was able to firmly fix the state of his heart and develop it steadily, more and more, bit by bit, without any decline or backsliding at all. Ajaan Mun used to goad him quite frequently. Any sign of self-indulgence and he would be scolded immediately. Ajaan Mun tended to become fierce and scold him much more quickly than before. His frequent exhortations and reminders were actually methods of helping Ajaan Khao to look after his *citta* and to maintain his level of Dhamma, for they made him more afraid of backsliding in his meditation.

From that time on, he continued to spend the *vassa* period with Ajaan Mun each year. After each *vassa*, he went out wandering in order to practise the way in places where he found it to be suitable for striving. Ajaan Mun would also go off wandering, but in a different direction so as to be on his own. He did not like wandering in the company of other Bhikkhus. So the Bhikkhus all went out in different directions, each as he felt inclined. But whenever some internal problem arose in their hearts, they would make for Ajaan Mun in order to ask for his advice. Each time he would explain the answer and clear up the problem.

Venerable Ajaan Khao's efforts in meditation continued to progress steadily. His mindfulness and wisdom gradually spread and branched out until they were infused into the heart so that they became one and the same with the heart. Whatever his bodily posture or activity, he maintained his effort with mindfulness and wisdom present at all times. His heart was bold and courageous. It had lost all fear of those things which arouse and maintain the thoughts and emotional states (*ārammaṇa*) that used to be his enemies. He was also certain of the path leading to freedom from *dukkha* — he had no doubts about it even though he had yet to actually attain complete freedom.

The Dhamma Remedy

When Venerable Ajaan Khao became ill while he was living in the forests and hills, he was never much concerned about finding medicines to cure himself. He tended to rely upon the 'Dhamma remedy' much more than any other method, for it was effective both for the body and for the *citta* at the same time. He would grasp the problem, fix his attention on it and reflect upon it for a long time — much longer than normal. Many times he managed to overcome fevers by this type of treatment, until he became quite confident of this technique of reflective investigation whenever he felt ill. It started from the time his *citta* attained *samādhi*, when his heart became calm and cool. Whenever he had a fever, he would set up a determination to fight it unwaveringly by meditating with a completely resolute heart — a method that had always brought him clearly visible results.

At first, when he had a fever he relied upon Venerable Ajaan Mun to guide him in the correct method. Ajaan Mun told him that whenever his own heart had gained unusually great strength, it nearly always came during times of severe sickness and pain. The more painful the sickness was, the more easily mindfulness and wisdom spun round and round the body, quickly going to each and every aspect of the illness as it happened. There was no need for him to compel himself to look into the body at that time. He had no interest at all in whether he got better or not. His only concern was to strive to know the truth of all the painful feelings as they arose and 'swooped down' on him at that time, using the mindfulness and wisdom that he had developed to expertise by continuous training.

Sometimes Venerable Ajaan Mun went to talk with Ajaan Khao when he had a fever. He tried to make him think by asking a pointed question, saying:

"Have you ever thought how in your past lives you experienced pain and suffering much more acute than this, just prior to the time you died? Even ordinary people in the world who have learnt nothing of Dhamma can put up with the suffering of an ordinary fever. Some of them even retain good mindfulness and seemly behaviour — better than many Bhikkhus. They do not groan and moan and restlessly move around, flinging their arms about while twisting and writhing, like some unworthy Bhikkhus who, really speaking, should not be Buddhists at all. Bhikkhus should never put themselves in a position where they tarnish the religion of the Buddha. Even though experiencing great pain and suffering, some lay people have enough mindfulness to control their manners so that they are seemly and respectable, which is quite admirable.

"I once saw a sick lay man whose children asked me to visit him as he was beyond hope of recovery. They said that their father wanted to meet me and pay his last respects to me, giving him something to keep in mind and to raise up his heart when he came to the time of his death. When I arrived at the house, no sooner had their father seen me walking up to the place where he was lying down, than he managed somehow to quickly sit up by himself, his face beaming and happy. He managed this in spite of his illness and in spite of the fact that normally he could not sit up without assistance. Actually, at that moment, all symptoms of his illness had disappeared, though there were enough indications left to show that he was quite seriously ill. He bowed down and paid homage with cheerfulness and joy in his heart, his manners and general behaviour being seemly and beautiful — which startled and perplexed everyone else in his home. They all wondered: 'How could he get up by himself? Normally, to move a little bit to a new position while lying prostrate we have to help him all the way with great care, fearing that otherwise he may be hurt or perhaps die right then. But as soon as he saw you coming, Venerable Ajaan, he got up like a new person — not like one who is about to die anytime.' They were amazed, for they had never seen anything like it before. Later they came to tell me that he died shortly after I left him. He was fully conscious right up to the last moment, and he seemed to die peacefully, as though he had reached some state of happiness.

"As for you, your illness is not as severe as that man's, so why are you so careless and unmindful about examining and investigating your situation. Or is it your laziness that weighs your heart down and makes your body weak and flabby. If many *Kammaṭṭhāna Bhikkhus* act like this, people will criticise the way of Buddhism. The way of *Kammaṭṭhāna* will fall apart because none of the Bhikkhus can put up with difficulties since they are all too weak and flabby. Their *Kammaṭṭhāna* is also weak and flabby, so they are just waiting on the chopping block for the *kilesas* to come and chop them up and make a salad of them. The Lord Buddha did not proclaim the teaching of mindfulness and wisdom for lazy, weak and flabby people who merely look at their sickness without thinking, searching and investigating in terms of Dhamma. The death of such a weak and lazy person would be of no consequence — in fact it's no more worthy than the death of a rat.

"Don't bring the attitude of a pig waiting casually on the 'chopping block' into the *Sāsana* and the circle of *Kammaṭṭhāna Bhikkhus*. It makes me feel ashamed in the face of those lay people who are more worthy than such Bhikkhus. I even feel ashamed in the face of the rats that die peacefully because they are better than Bhikkhus who become weak and lazy when they have a fever, and then die without any mindfulness and wisdom to look after themselves. You should try doing some investigation to see whether the Dhamma truths — such as the Truth of *Dukkha* — are really true or not. How true are they, and where is their truth to be found? Does the truth dwell in the carelessness, weakness and laziness that you are promoting at present? These tendencies are just promoting the Cause of *Dukkha* so that it accumulates in the *citta*, making you stupid and preventing you from rising out of it. It is not the way of the Path — which leads one entirely to the Cessation of *Dukkha*.

"I boldly proclaim that I have gained strength of heart at times of severe sickness by examining the *dukkha* that arose within me. I saw clearly the place where it arose and established itself, along with its dying away and ceasing, by means of true mindfulness and wisdom. The *citta* that knows the Truth of *Dukkha* becomes calm and peaceful. It does not go about looking for something to change its state; instead, being 'one' and single, it remains firmly within the truth. There is nothing in the *citta* to cause trouble or unseemly actions; nor can anything false enter to cause doubt or uncertainty. At that point, painful feelings either cease completely or, even if they remain, they are quite unable to overwhelm the *citta*. The *citta* and the pain are both true, each in its own sphere[8]. This is where the Dhamma Truths become the highest truths. You must stay focused in the *citta* as you thoroughly investigate everything. Mindfulness and wisdom become active because you investigate, not because you're too lazy to make use of the very tools that are capable of countering the *kilesas*.

"Here is a simile to help you understand: If you take a stone and throw it at someone's head, it can cause injury, or maybe even kill him. But you can also make valuable use of that stone for sharpening knives, or other purposes. Accordingly, a fool uses a stone to do damage, whereas a clever person uses it for good purposes to help himself in desirable ways. Mindfulness and wisdom are like this: they can be used wrongly to think out ways of doing things that are morally bad; such as, being clever in a deceitful way in one's business affairs, or clever in robbery and banditry, or being slick and quicker than a monkey so that others cannot follow what one is up to — all actions that usually turn into evil because of using mindfulness and wisdom in the wrong way.

"But we can also use mindfulness and wisdom in the right way in our livelihood, by using them in such things as building work, or carpentry, or writing, or the various kinds of repair work in which we are skilled. Or we may use them to cure our *kilesas* and *taṅhā* — which fix us firmly to the wheel of *saṁsāra* and lead us to endless rounds of birth and death — until they have all been removed from the heart. Then we become purified and reach the state of freedom, *Nibbāna*. It may happen today, or this month, or this year, or in this lifetime; for it is not beyond the ability of human beings to attain this, as we can see from the example of those clever people who have done so from the time of the Lord Buddha up to the present day.

"Wisdom brings endless benefits to those who have enough interest and incentive to use contemplative thought without fixing any bounds or limits to it. Mindfulness and wisdom have never deceived people by leading them into a state of despair with no way out. So we need not be afraid that we'll develop too much mindfulness and wisdom, or that they will turn us into someone who is good at breaking up and destroying whatever Dhamma we have within us. We need not fear that an abundance of mindfulness and wisdom will hinder our chances of attaining freedom by overwhelming us before we're even half way there.

"Since ancient times, the wisest of people have always praised mindfulness and wisdom, saying that they are the most exalted faculties, and never out-of-date. You should therefore think and search, digging up mindfulness and wisdom and promoting them as the best means of defending yourself and the best method of completely destroying the enemy within you. Then you will see a most excellent and precious sphere of the heart that has always been there within you since endless ages past. This Dhamma that I am teaching to you comes entirely from the Dhamma that I have experienced directly as a result of investigating it thoroughly. It is not based on guess-work — like scratching without being able to locate the itch — for what I teach comes from what I have known and experienced with certainty.

"Those who want to get free from *dukkha*, yet are afraid of the *dukkha* that arises within them and so refuse to investigate it, will never be able to get free from *dukkha*. The way to *Nibbāna* depends on the Truth of *Dukkha* and the Cause of *Dukkha* as the means of going forward on the Path. *The Lord Buddha and every one of the Sāvaka Arahants attained the fulfilment of the Path, Fruition and Nibbāna by means of the Four Noble Truths.* Not one of them failed to pass completely through these Noble Truths.

"At this time some of these Noble Truths are quite clearly and openly displaying their true nature within your body and mind. You must investigate these truths, using mindfulness and wisdom to get to really know them clearly. You must not sit back and merely gaze at them or you will become an invalid in the area of these Dhamma Truths which have always been true since the beginning of the world.

"If we *Dhutanga Kammaṭṭhāna Bhikkhus* cannot face the truth that is displaying itself so clearly to us, who else will ever be able to face up to it and know it? Those in *Kammaṭṭhāna* circles are closer and more intimate with the Dhamma Truths than anyone else, so they should be able to realise their true nature before others do. Although others outside the circle of *Kammaṭṭhāna* also have the Dhamma Truths as an inherent part of the body and mind, they differ in that they avoid doing any investigation which would lead them to understand them in a different way. This is because their position as lay people affords them less of an opportunity to pursue these practices.

"But the *Dhutanga Kammaṭṭhāna Bhikkhu* is a special case, for he is fully prepared to progress steadily towards realising the truth which is apparent within him all the time. If you have the blood of a warrior who is truly worthy of the name given by the Great Teacher — *Sākyaputta Buddhajinorasa* (Son of the *Sākya*, the Victorious Buddha) — you must try to investigate so as to realise the truth clearly.

"Right now the truth about painful feeling is announcing its presence within your body and mind in a clear and unmistakable manner. Don't let the opportunity presented to you by this pain pass by uselessly. Instead, I want you to extract the truth from that painful feeling and bring it up for mindfulness and wisdom to analyse. Then mark it well, so that it makes an indelible impression on your heart. From then on, it will act as an example to show that you have now gained a clear understanding of this first of the four Truths that the Lord Buddha proclaimed throughout his teaching, namely, the Truth of *Dukkha*. You will have gained this understanding by means of your mindfulness and wisdom in a way that leaves no room for doubt. This will happen as you endeavour to make knowledge of that Truth steadily develop, thus increasing your understanding until every bit of doubt has disappeared.

"If you strive to do what I have just taught you, then although the fever in your body increases, you yourself will appear to be perfectly well and fit. In other words, your heart won't be disturbed by or apprehensive of the pain arising in your body. Instead, you will take pride and satisfaction from what you have realised in a calm, steady manner. You will not display any outward symptoms, restlessly moving and changing about as the fever gets worse. This is what's meant by learning Dhamma for the Truth. The wisest people have all learnt it in this way. They do not wishfully imagine the types of feelings they would like to have — thinking how they would prefer this or that kind of feeling according to their desires — all of which merely accumulates the Cause of *Dukkha*, thus making it increase and grow much stronger.

"You must take this teaching to heart and remember it well. You must continue investigating to find the meaning of Dhamma, which is the Truth that is within yourself. This knowledge is well within each and every person's capability. I am merely the one who teaches the way to do it. Whether the pupil is fearless and valiant, or weak and flabby, depends entirely on the person who does the investigation — no one else has a say in that at all. Well now! It's time for you to live up to your teacher's expectations. Don't just lie there like a foot-wiping rag, letting the *kilesas* come to stomp all over you and beat you out flat. This would be disastrous and bring nothing but trouble in the future — don't say I haven't warned you!"

Venerable Ajaan Khao recalled that: "When Venerable Ajaan Mun gave me this Dhamma talk, it was as though a violent storm had passed through and then disappeared. I was so moved by his skilful, penetrating teaching that I felt I would float up into the air with rapture and joy. Nothing else could have been so valuable to me at that time. As soon as Ajaan Mun left, I began practising the methods in which he had so kindly instructed me. I began to the best of my ability to examine and unravel the problem of the painful feelings I was experiencing then, without exhibiting any form of weakness at all.

"While doing the investigation of pain after Ajaan Mun left, it felt as if he were still sitting there with me, watching me and waiting to help show me how to do it the whole time. More than that, the feeling of his presence gave me strength of heart to increase my fight with painful feeling.

"While doing the investigation, I tried to separate *dukkha* out from the *khandhas*. In other words, the body and all its parts I put into one heap *(khandha)*; *saññā* (memory), which stands by to define or determine, thereby deceiving us, I divided into a second heap; *sankhāra*, which is thinking and imagining, I put into a third heap; and the *citta* I put separately into a special category. Then I investigated, I compared, I looked for causes and results from the arising and ceasing of the chaotic jumble of pain that was racking my body. But I did not think about whether the pain would die away and I would survive, or whether it would get worse and I would die, for I was absolutely determined to get to know the truth of all these things.

"In particular, I wanted to find out what in fact the Truth of *Dukkha* was. Why should it have such power that it can shake up and disturb the hearts of all beings throughout the world without exception? This happens when *dukkha* arises in normal circumstances due to all sorts of different causes. More so, it arises when people reach the end of their lives and are just about to leave this life and go to a new state. All sentient beings of every kind feel very frightened at that time. None of them are bold and fearless enough to face up to death and accept it — except when they are forced to face it because there's no other alternative, no way out. If there was any way to avoid it, they would escape to the other end of the world if necessary to get away from it — all because of the fear of death.

"After Ajaan Mun left, I thought to myself: 'I am also one of these sentient beings who are timid and frightened of *dukkha*, so what should I do about the *dukkha* I'm now experiencing in order that I may be bold and fearless, with the truth as my witness. Well! I must contend with *dukkha* by using mindfulness and wisdom to follow the methods taught by the Great Teacher, and my own teacher as well. A short time ago, Venerable Ajaan Mun kindly taught me in a way that went straight to my heart, leaving no room for doubt. He taught that I should fight using mindfulness and wisdom to separate and analyse these *khandhas*, examining to see them quite clearly. Right now, what *khandha* is this painful feeling? Can it be the body, or memory, or thought and imagination, or consciousness, or the *citta*? If it cannot be any of those, then why do I make out that the painful feeling is me — that I am in pain— that pain is truly mine? Am I really this painful feeling, or what? I must find out the truth of this today. So, if the pain does not stop, and I have not come to know this painful feeling quite clearly with true mindfulness and wisdom, I shall go on sitting here in meditation until I die if necessary. But I will definitely not get up from this place just to let the pain mock and ridicule me.'

"From that moment on, mindfulness and wisdom began aggressively analysing as if it were a matter of life or death. This life-and-death struggle between the *citta* and the pain went on for five hours. Following that, I knew the truth about each one of the *khandhas* on its own. But in particular, I knew the feeling group most clearly by means of wisdom. *As soon as the investigation had thoroughly and completely penetrated every aspect of the khandhas, the painful feelings died away immediately. From then on, an unshakeable faith in the validity of the Noble Truths arose in me, based upon the Truth of Dukkha. I then knew the truth of it without any doubt or uncertainty.*

"From that day forward, whenever I got a fever, or any other sickness, my heart was able to be victorious by practising the way of mindfulness and wisdom — never again was I weak and spineless in the face of pain. Instead, my heart gained strength in times of pain and sickness, which are times of serious concern — maybe even matters of life and death. The Dhamma which I, like most ordinary people not faced with a critical situation, had never taken very seriously, then displayed the truth for me to see clearly as I thoroughly investigated painful feeling. The pain then ceased, and the heart became concentrated and went down and reached the base of *samādhi*. All doubts and problems with regard to the body and mind then ceased while they went quiescent. This lasted until the *citta* withdrew from that state, which took several hours. Whatever else needed to be investigated would be dealt with in the future with fearless regard for the Truth which had already been seen."

When Ajaan Khao's *citta* became concentrated and dropped down to reach the basis of *samādhi* due to the powerful influence of the investigation, the fever ceased immediately and did not return again. He said that it was quite extraordinary how this could happen.

In regard to this, the author believes what Ajaan Khao said without question, because I have also done such investigations in a similar manner and have experienced the same kind of results. So I feel fully confident that the 'Dhamma remedy' is quite capable of treating sickness in subtle and strange ways, and I appreciate those meditators who have tendencies of character in this direction.

Most of the *Dhutanga Kammaṭṭhāna Bhikkhus* like to do such investigations as a remedy for their own body and mind when they become seriously ill with painful fevers. But they like doing it quietly on their own, and they don't readily tell other people about it — except their friends who are also doing the practice in the same way and who have similar characters. With them they can talk intimately about these things.

It must be understood, however, that the aforementioned practice of curing diseases by using meditation should not be taken to mean that all diseases can be cured by such methods. Even the Bhikkhus who practice them are by no means sure which diseases can be cured in this way and which cannot. But regardless of what happens, they are never indifferent or neglectful about the changes taking place within them. Even when it happens that the body is going to die due to a disease, they must also use the power of the 'Dhamma remedy' to make sure that some of the diseases of the *citta* — meaning some of the *kilesas* and *āsavas* — die at the same time. They are therefore relentless in their investigations into the various diseases that arise, both in the body and in the *citta*. They believe it to be an important and necessary duty in connection with the *khandhas* and the *citta* — which they must investigate and accept responsibility for, right up to the last moment.

VENERABLE AJAAN KHAO invariably preferred to cure fevers and illnesses by using the 'Dhamma remedy'. At one time he was staying in a hilly part of Sakon Nakhon province which at that time was infested with malaria. One day after he had finished eating his food, he immediately began to feel feverish and shivery. He wrapped himself in several blankets to keep warm, but to no avail. He looked about for a warm place but it was hopeless, so he gave up trying to treat the problem by external means. He decided, instead, to treat it internally by means of Dhamma, which he had already done successfully in the past. He told the other Bhikkhus who were with him to go away and leave him alone. They were to wait until they saw that he had opened the door of his hut before coming to see him again. After all the Bhikkhus had gone, he began to meditate by investigating painful feelings in the same way as he had done before. He started about 9 o'clock in the morning and went on until 3 o'clock in the afternoon before he was finally successful. The fever died away and he was cured. At the same time, his *citta* became concentrated and dropped down until it reached its natural level, where it rested for about two hours. Finally, at about 6 o'clock in the evening, he left the place where he had been practising *samādhi* meditation, feeling a buoyancy of body and heart without anything left to cause him trouble. The fever had completely gone and his *citta* had become bright and skilled with wisdom, standing out prominently within himself. He has lived with the *Vihāra-dhamma*[9] ever since then.

Locked in Spiritual Combat

While Ajaan Khao was spending the *vassa* at Wat Pa Ban
Poang, Sun Maha Pon district in Chiang Mai province, he
accelerated his efforts in meditation round the clock in every
posture and activity, much more so than in his previous *vassa*
periods. In previous years he had worked very hard as well,
but this *vassa* he made a special effort beyond what he had
done before. He did this by maintaining his efforts in the three
postures of standing, walking and sitting, without lying down
at all. If he slept at all, he did so in the sitting position he used
when doing *samādhi bhāvanā*, and only then when his body and
mind had reached the limit of their ability to go without sleep
— which was a time when his mindfulness was at a low ebb.
But he refused to let himself give up working so as to lie down
and sleep, as he used to when he indulged in the forth posture
of lying down. This was because he clearly saw good results in
both *samādhi* and wisdom. He saw how his heart was more intimately calm and his wisdom was more subtle, penetrating and
proficient than when he was striving in the way he had been
practising before. This gave him encouragement in his effort
to maintain the practice in the three postures throughout the
vassa without letting his body slouch or assume a posture that
would incline towards lying down to sleep.

If we use the language of a warrior, he was locked in combat, fighting to win or lose against the *kilesas*, which like to
think only of a comfortable bed and a pillow. If they had their
way, he would lie down and give in completely, laid out flat at

full length like a snake — together with his faith, effort, mindfulness, *samādhi* and wisdom.

So he determined that those *kilesas* which drag the Bhikkhu down onto the sleeping mat must put up with fasting (Bhikkhu meat is tasty for the *kilesas*) and emaciation for those three months of the *vassa* period. Then those five Dhamma-results would get a chance to walk along the path of the Lord Buddha. Practising in that way, he could sense imminent victory coming from his struggle to fight in all three postures, as though he were on the verge of attaining Dhamma in each posture. This added increased enthusiasm to his efforts. His body and heart became light and buoyant due to the various kinds of Dhamma he developed, and his striving became easier as it shifted back and forth fighting against the *kilesas*. He was not concerned about the difficulties he faced in fighting the *kilesas*, which he realised deep in his heart were his enemies.

ONE NIGHT WHILE HE WAS SITTING in *samādhi bhāvanā*, his *citta* dropped down into a subtle state of calm and reached the ground of *samādhi*. It remained there resting for a long time before withdrawing to the level of *upacāra samādhi*, where a *nimitta* arose in his *citta* and he saw the whole earth whirling round like a wheel. The more closely he examined that *nimitta*, the faster it went round, as though the earth and sky were about to collapse. He felt as though he was floating just above the ground and moving along parallel with the earth, though he wasn't actually walking. In the *nimitta* it seemed that his body was floating along the *caṅkama* path he normally used. It floated back and forth many times before it stopped. As soon as it stopped, a light appeared. It seemed to shine down from the sky above and enter into his heart, enabling him to see all the parts within his body quite clearly. He became engrossed in examining the various parts within his body, contemplating them in terms of the 'basis for the seeing of their loathsomeness' (*asubha kammaṭṭhāna*) and in terms of the 'three character- istics' (*Ti-lakkaṇa*), and the heart was joyful and bright with wisdom, faith and fearless determination.

He discovered many skilful ways and methods for ex- tracting various kinds of *kilesas*, methods that came to him continually throughout that retreat period. During that *vassa* he practised with great energy and enthusiasm and he under- stood things very clearly. He experienced none of the sombre moods that had troubled him often in the past. Instead, there was a firm resolve in the direction of *samādhi*, and a clever skilfulness and nimbleness in the direction of mindfulness and wisdom, those two friends of a heart that's striving relentlessly in every posture. At that level, the relationship between mind- fulness and wisdom and the *citta*, which is known as 'automatic striving', began to appear quite clearly within the *citta*. Then, in all postures, the *citta* kept up a constant effort all the time, excepting only when he slept. There was no longer a need to force mindfulness and wisdom to work like there had been in the past when he was forced to push them to strive all the time. Previously, if he had not done so, the *kilesas* would have forced him onto the 'chopping block' where he would never have been able to stand against them. At earlier stages of his training, his *kilesas* were much more active, quick and penetrating than his mindfulness, wisdom and effort were.

We should never pride ourselves on being really clever and skilled when the *citta* is merely at the level of *samādhi*, or calmness. Although the *citta* is calm, it is still subject to the seductive temptations of the *kilesas*, which cause it to become addicted to *samādhi* and so lose all interest in investigating with wisdom — which is the way to extract the *kilesas* and get rid of them from the heart.

When the time comes that wisdom moves out to do the work of confronting and fighting the various *kilesas*, it steadily succeeds in defeating them, rarely finding that it is at a loss, not knowing what to do. We steadily get to know the various alluring enticements of the *kilesas* — how they appear so harmoniously beautiful and melodious that we become overwhelmed by their lingering appeal. This is why all beings in the world never tire of the various enticements used by the *kilesas*. This despite the fact that they tempt beings over and over again to love, and to hate, and to be so angry or greedy as to cause beings great difficulty because they have to put up with so much suffering and torment. However many hundreds, or thousands, or millions of times people do this, still they are never fed up or satiated with it; nor do they see the harmfulness of these enticements at all. If they do see the harm in them, it comes only in a flash when they are experiencing so much suffering and torment that they are truly in a corner with no way out. But almost immediately the allure of the *kilesas* returns and puts them into a dozing sleep. From then on, the day never comes when anything arouses them enough to see the harmfulness of it.

The effort that begins arising at this level of practice is an aggressive kind of effort which fights the *kilesas*, repeatedly striking at them in many different ways so as to beat up and kill off more and more of them. This kind of effort is in no way at a loss, because it is not lulled into a drunken stupor by the *kilesas*. It does not look on them as friends and allies and so submit to them in life and death, as was the case before the Dhamma weapons of mindfulness and wisdom were powerful enough to overwhelm them. At the stage that Ajaan Khao had reached, all of his Dhamma weapons were becoming very powerful as they shone forth brightly. They really enjoyed digging up the *kilesas*, pulling them out and tearing them to pieces quite ruthlessly.

It seems that the firmness of his intention to gain that realm where there is freedom from *dukkha* steadily gained strength until his striving reached a point of urgency where the practice was a matter of life and death. Whatever was good would remain, whatever was bad must be destroyed without any regrets. Birth and death are barbs and thorns which the *kilesas* always stab into the heart, where they have been the ruling power for countless ages. But they were no longer allowed to have any power to rule, for from then on it was to be the supremely excellent pure Dhamma which alone had power to rule over the heart. Dhamma now ruled the heart where Ajaan Khao previously let the *kilesas* and the 'wheel of *saṁsāra*' rule. Instead of Dhamma being driven away and losing out to the *kilesas* every time, he refused to have the *kilesas* in his heart anymore.

AFTER THAT VASSA PERIOD, he left that place to go wandering in the *Kammaṭṭhāna* way wherever he felt like going. He went to stay near a forest village in Chiang Mai province where a small hut had been built. In the past, *Dhutanga Kammaṭṭhāna Bhikkhus* had stayed there to work at their practice, but now it was abandoned. It was a very peaceful and quiet place, far away from the village, so he stayed there to develop his practice.

One day it started raining heavily in the middle of the day, so he could not go out to walk *caṅkama*. He closed the door, the windows and the wall[10], and he sat in *bhāvanā* on the floor of the hut, which was raised well above the ground.

While he was sitting doing meditation, it seemed to him that a red-hot burning pipe had been stuck into his butt. It stopped for awhile and then came up again. So he turned to investigate what it was all about. As soon as his *citta* turned to focus on the cause of the hot pipe which was burning him, he realised that the fire was actually the heat of sexual desire appearing from beneath his hut. He knew that it did not come from his own heart. He checked his investigation thoroughly and confirmed that it was in fact the fire of *rāgataṅhā* coming from underneath his hut, for in his own *citta* there was absolutely no sign of *rāgataṅhā* at all.

The whole time he was engaged in investigating this fire, he never paused to wonder where this fire came from. He was merely reflecting internally trying to work out in his heart: "How has this blaze of *rāga* been able to cling onto me? I have no fixed attachment to or desire for any man or woman, so my heart is normal — no *rāga* has arisen in it."

Every day when he went on *piṇḍapāta* in the village, he went fully self-controlled, having mindfulness present to watch cautiously every aspect and phase of all those emotional biases which had been enemies of the *citta*. His heart could never find any aspect of *rāgataṅhā* that could be an emotional bias.

When that 'fire' had calmed down and no longer showed itself, he opened his eyes and rose from his meditation seat, by which time the rain had stopped. Looking behind him, he saw a woman come out from under his hut and walk away. This made him connect the fire that had burned him with the woman who was just then walking away from under his hut. He realised then that the woman probably had bad thoughts about him, which caused that incident to happen. It's something that he would never have imagined possible.

Actually that woman was quite young, about 25 years old, and most likely unmarried. She was probably out gathering edible plants or firewood, for she was carrying a basket. As she approached his hut it started to rain heavily, so she quickly took shelter under the hut until the rain stopped, after which she came out and walked away. When Ajaan Khao looked out the window, which was covered by a straw mat with many gaps in it, he could see the woman quite clearly.

When telling this story to the Bhikkhus and novices on suitable occasions, Ajaan Khao never implied that he was blaming or criticising the woman at all. He simply used the story of this woman as an example to explain to them about the flow of the *citta*. Whether focused externally or internally, it is something so subtle that we are normally unaware of it. It is only the process of investigation in the manner of the practice of *citta bhāvanā* that enables us to gradually come to know such things.

He said that his *citta* was in a very subtle state at that time, and his mindfulness and wisdom were fast enough to keep up with such happenings. They were not as slow as they used to be when he first started to train himself, so when the *rāga* within his *citta* suddenly became active his mindfulness kept up with it, but his wisdom was still not able to cut it off at that stage. Later on, the ability of mindfulness and wisdom that he trained relentlessly reached the point where *rāga* could not stand against it, so it was bound to break up and disperse from the heart in a clearly evident way.

He felt at that stage that his striving was progressing very quickly and fearlessly. When performing the regular morning and evening chanting, he did it in a brief form, for his mind was in a hurry to get on to striving with mindfulness and wisdom. He even stopped reciting the various *sutta* texts, which he previously chanted, in order to put all his effort into developing his mindfulness and wisdom so as to gain freedom as quickly as possible while there was still time. He was afraid that he would die before he got to his desired goal — the *Arahatta-dhamma*.

above: Ajaan Khao seated in front of Cave of the Midday Drum; *top right:* Ajaan Khao (far right) presiding over the Kathina robe-offering ceremony inside the cave; *bottom right:* receiving offerings of cloth from devoted supporters.

Ajaan Khao was eminently
qualified to be a constant
source of merit for those in
the world who associated
with him. His outward
behaviour was impeccable,
while his spiritual attainment
was like a diamond of the
first water buried deep
within his heart.

When Ajaan Khao lived in the forests and the mountains, he got the local villagers to lay out three different paths for walking meditation. He walked caṅkama on these three paths at three different times each day.

In the early afternoon, he started walking on the path dedicated to Dhamma Pūjā.

Path Two

Dhamma Pūjā

The Completely Pure Citta

A bad fever afflicted Ajaan Khao the following *vassa*, but his relentless efforts against the *kilesas* continued. Neither side would back down. The fever remained with him throughout the *vassa*, but his examination of the painful feelings and the body — which is the home of suffering — never weakened or gave way. However strong the fever and however much the suffering, it was as though they acted as fuel for mindfulness and wisdom, causing them to show their skilfulness to the utmost. His heart took up the pain that arose from the fever in his body, which was the basis of his suffering, and used those painful feelings like a boxing ring to stage a fight against the *kilesas*, which were so punishing they gave no break for rest at the end of each round. If mindfulness and wisdom had relaxed or given way, the fever would have lay him out cold, and probably have kill him. So he and his *kilesas* fought together in the manner of a life-or-death struggle. Neither the fever nor his suffering eased or gave way at all, so his striving could not give way either. If he gave way, he could not keep up with the *kilesas* and destroy them. So the outcome depended on his diligent effort. As there was no way he could avoid the situation, he was forced to keep on struggling until he understood the reasons behind his suffering. Only then was he able to be victorious and gain confidence in his ability.

That *vassa* was extremely difficult. Because he suffered malarial fever throughout the whole retreat period, he was required to push himself to the limit, both physically and mentally. The physical pain was excruciating; while in his heart he was striving relentlessly to follow the fever and the painful feelings.

After the end of the *vassa*, his fever gradually subsided and went away. He then left and went wandering in solitude, going from place to place as it suited his inclinations without attachment to anything except only his efforts in meditation. It was then the season when the rice was harvested.

One evening after he swept the ground around his hut, he went off to take a bath. As he was walking along, he saw how the rice growing in the fields was golden yellow and almost ripe. This immediately made him think and question:

"This rice has sprouted and grown because there is a seed which caused it to grow. The heart that endlessly leads one to birth and death must also have something that acts as a seed within it in the same way the rice plants have. If that seed in the heart is not destroyed entirely, it is bound to lead to further births and deaths going on endlessly. Now, what is this seed in the heart? What could it be but the *kilesas*, *avijjā*, *taṇhā* and *upādāna*?"

He continued thinking and probing into this problem, taking *avijjā* as the target of his research. He investigated it by going forward and then backward, backward and then forward, examining it over and over again with intense interest, trying to understand the true nature of *avijjā*. Beginning at dusk and

continuing throughout the night, he went on relentlessly investigating the relationship between *avijjā* and the *citta. At dawn,
just as it was beginning to get light, his wisdom was able to break
through to a final conclusion. Avijjā then fell away from the citta
without any remainder. The contemplation of the rice stopped at
the point where the rice was ripe never to sprout again. His investigation into the citta also stopped as soon as avijjā ceased, after
which the citta became ripe in the same way as the rice became
ripe. At that point it was clearly evident to him that the citta had
stopped creating any more births in the various realms of existence.*
What remained for him to admire to his complete satisfaction,
as he sat in his hut in the midst of the mountains, was the complete and utter purity of the *citta*.

At the moment the *citta* passed beyond the tangled
jungles of the 'round of *kilesas*' (*kilesa-vaṭṭa*), wonder and
amazement arose in him as he sat alone at dawn. Then the
sun began to shine brightly in the sky, while his heart began
to get brighter and brighter as it left the realm of *avijjā* and
went towards the wonder of Dhamma where it reached
vimutti — freedom — as the sun rose above the mountains. It
was truly a most auspicious and wonderful occasion.

After this supremely auspicious and blessed moment had
passed, it was time for him to go *piṇḍapāta*. While he was
walking away from that auspicious place, he looked back at
the little hut that had provided him with so much happiness
and such wonders. Then, looking all around him, he saw how
everything else appeared to have become supremely auspicious
in sympathy with his heart, which was entirely and completely

wonderful throughout — although, in fact, all these things were simply there in accordance with their own nature as usual.

While walking on *piṇḍapāta*, his heart was filled with Dhamma. When he looked at the local forest people who had looked after him, it seemed almost as if they were all divine beings. He reflected on all the assistance they had so graciously given him, and he felt that it would be impossible to describe the extent of their virtue. *Mettā* and compassion arose in him for those 'heavenly' forest people. He could not help but spread out the *mettā* in his *citta* as a dedication to them as he passed by them along the route, which he did until he reached the vicinity of the hut where he stayed, which was a place of such happiness.

While he arranged the simple food which the hill people had put into his bowl, his heart was full of Dhamma. He did not turn his thoughts to the food that had always sustained his body, but he merely ate it as that which the body depended upon for its maintenance. He later recalled:

"Since the day I was born this was the first time that I had ever experienced the body and mind in perfect harmony with the *citta*, which is something quite impossible to explain. All I can say is that it was a most wonderful and unique experience that became the most outstanding event of my life, leaving a deep and lasting impression on my heart.

"After this world-shaking event occurred, when the sky and ground collapsed and the 'wheel of *saṁsāra*' — the *vaṭṭa-cakka* in the heart — broke up and disappeared, all the elements and *khandhas* as well as every part and aspect of the *citta* were all free to conform to their own natural state. They were no longer enslaved or forced into service by anything. The five *indriya* and the six *āyatana* will continue to function and do their duties until they disappear at death, but there won't be any dispute between them as there was in the past. (The dispute he referred to is the disharmony between internal sense bases and external objects when they come into contact. This contact in turn gives rise to gladness or sorrow that then turns into the arising of *sukha* and *dukkha*. All these are interconnected like the links of an endless chain going on forever.)

"The disputes within the *citta*, which are far more numerous and disturbing than those externally in the world, all stopped at the moment the 'court of justice' was finally established within the heart. Such troublesome disputes used to take the *citta* as the arena where they would dance about arguing and quarrelling. The *citta* was never given any time to be calm and quiet, because *avijjā-taṅhā*, 'the boss', directed and ordered it to cause turmoil and confusion of countless different kinds. But now, all of that has dissolved into a joyful harmonious state of peaceful calm. The world within the *citta* is now free and empty. Now only the most superb and excellent Truths of Dhamma (*Vijjā-Dhamma*) are produced there, which allows me to enjoy the realm of the '*citta*-king' instead of the former state of anti-Dhamma.

"Affairs, both external and internal, now proceed smoothly in accordance with Dhamma without being harassed and disturbed by an enemy. So the eyes see, the ears hear, the nose smells, the tongue tastes, the body feels things hot or cold, soft or hard, and the heart receives and knows the various supporters of perceptions (*ārammaṇa*) in its natural way without distorting and altering everything as it used to — making out that right is wrong, that being shackled is freedom, that what is bad is good, that ghosts are people, that virtuous Bhikkhus are evil ghosts *(preta)* and conversely that evil ghosts are good people. That is what the Lord of anti-Dhamma used to do when he had the power to dictate. Now I can simply sit down and rest peacefully, knowing that whether I live or die I have complete happiness. I am genuinely free of *dukkha* and free of danger without any residue of attachment of any sort whatsoever."

This was the aphorism that Venerable Ajaan Khao exclaimed in his heart at that time.

AJAAN KHAO WAS ONE OF SEVERAL of Venerable Ajaan Mun's disciples who stripped away all *dukkha* and got rid of all dangers from his heart while living and practising in Chiang Mai province. He said:

"The place where I practised the way until I reached freedom from the *dukkha* within me made a strong impression on me. There was the little hut which gave me shelter so I could practise and strive and also rest my body; the paths where I walked *caṅkama*; the place where I sat in *samādhi* meditation day and night; and the village where I walked for *piṇḍapāta* to get food for maintaining my body. All of them made a great impression that went deep into my heart in an inexplicable way, far more so than any other place I ever lived at. This feeling has remained buried in my heart right up to the present day, and my memory of that place has never faded or become dull and stale. From the moment when the 'wheel of *saṃsāra*' was demolished and fell away from my heart, that place changed and became the abode of supreme happiness in all situations at all times. It was as if I were in the presence of the Lord Buddha at the place of his enlightenment, and every other place where he practised striving for Dhamma.

"All uncertainty about the Lord Buddha was swept away at that moment. Even though he entered *Parinibbāna* a long time ago, as reckoned by the usual conventions of time, yet it seems as though he is residing here in my heart every moment, as though he had never entered *Parinibbāna* at all. All of my uncertainties about the true nature of Dhamma — whether it is much or little, profound or shallow, gross or subtle — were entirely swept away. I understood that Dhamma is permanently established in this one heart and that this Dhamma is complete in and of itself without any deficiencies whatsoever. All doubt and uncertainty disappeared concerning the *Sāvaka Sangha*, which is *Supaṭipanno*. These three 'Jewels' of absolute purity are fused into one in the heart that lives with Buddha, Dhamma and Sangha, each of which are pure and integrated together as one Dhamma.

"From that time on, I have remained completely contented with no concerns or worries deceiving my heart. Whatever my circumstances, I am my own master in that situation. Nothing remains to order me about or to creep in and ask for a share of everything — like a parasite — as when I was living with that beggar all the time, without realising it. First it wanted this! Then it wanted that! It was always pleading for something."

When Ajaan Khao spoke of 'wanting this' and 'wanting that', he was talking about the *kilesas*, whose basic nature is to always feel needy and unsatisfied. Once they have established a powerful position in the heart of a person or animal, they are bound to demand or beg incessantly, for this is their natural way of acting. They constantly incite us to think like this, or to speak like that, or to act in various ways according to their power. If we don't have the Dhamma needed to prevent the 'leakage' which comes from the stubborn demanding and begging of this gang of *kilesas*, we are likely to be divided up as spoils so that they can 'eat us up', until there is nothing left.

It can even reach the point where we don't have enough virtue left to enable us to be born again in the future as a good person with moral principles. Wherever we are reborn, it is bound to be the wrong place and the wrong situation. We won't be able to get sufficient contentment in our next birth to justify the effort we made to be born into such a state. Then we will have lost not only our 'capital', but the 'interest' from it as well. In other words, when we are heedless and complacent, we grant the *kilesas* the power to take complete charge of the *citta*, without having any defence to resist them at all. They then take over and grab until there's nothing left.

But those who get rid of all their debts, and put an end to the untidy mess in their hearts, continue to live happily in all the activities of their *khandhas*. When life comes to an end, they drop the burden of the *khandhas*. All that remains is the purity of "Buddho". This is the complete and eternal end of all *dukkha* — a wonderful ending, and a moment of far greater value than anything in the three worlds. It is quite different from existence in the world of conventions (*sammuti*) where most beings openly desire birth, and are not in the least interested to consider the *dukkha* which is bound to come as a consequence of that birth.

The truth is that birth and *dukkha* cannot be separated. Even in those cases where it is minimal, *dukkha* is still bound to be there. The wisest of men are therefore far more afraid of birth than they are of death. By contrast, most of us fear death more than birth. But death is simply a result of its basic cause, which is birth. This fear of death is a fear that is in complete opposition to the basic principles of nature, and it comes about because people have no interest in searching out the truth about death. Indeed they resist it, so *dukkha* is with them all the time.

If the wisest of men had the kind of *kilesas* that made them laugh at other's foolishness, they would probably be unable to contain themselves and may have to let it all out to their heart's content when they see almost everyone in the world setting themselves against the truth with such determination — without ever looking around to search for the basic principles of truth. But actually the truly wise do not act in the usual way of the world. They have only *mettā* and compassion for the world, giving help by teaching the way. As for those who are beyond all hope, the wise let them go their way as nothing can be done to help them.

VENERABLE AJAAN KHAO TRANSCENDED all the fear and danger that he used to have in *saṁsāra* and reached *Nibbāna* while still alive *(Sa-upādisesa-nibbāna)* when living in a place called Long Khot in the Phrao district of Chiang Mai province, in his sixteenth or seventeenth *vassa*. I cannot remember which, but I do know that it was the beginning of the harvest season just after the end of the *vassa* period. He related the whole story to me in a manner that touched the heart, one evening as we discussed Dhamma from 8 p.m. until after midnight. Because nobody came to disturb us for the whole of that time, both of us were able to talk Dhamma freely, right through to the final conclusion — which was the final result that arose from our practice of Dhamma. We started from the basic ABCs of our respective practices, which meant the basic training that we did which was a mixture of slipping back and scrambling up again, at times falling into a bad state, or a state that alternated between bad and good, and at other times feeling the satisfaction or dejection which resulted from the ups and downs of the practices that we used in our initial training. We went on right through our meditation until we each reached the ultimate and final point of the *citta* and Dhamma.

The results of my discussion with him were so satisfying that I have taken the opportunity to include his comments in this book so that those who read it and are interested in attaining Dhamma may use it as a field for contemplation. They can then choose which aspects are suitable for them to use in their own practice, depending on their own temperaments. The result which comes from such a discriminating choice is likely to be a smooth and steady development that is right and appropriate, depending on the strength of one's resolve.

Ajaan Khao was entirely qualified to be a constant source of great value for those in the world who associated with him. His outward behaviour was impeccable, as was his inward knowing of the way of Dhamma, which was like a 'diamond of the first water' buried deeply within him. Such a precious gem is extremely hard to find, and can only be found by someone who has returned from the threshold of death. I have secretly given him the name: "Diamond of the First Water" in the *Kammaṭṭhāna* linage of Venerable Ajaan Mun without being afraid that people will call me mad — because this arose from my own faith.

Return to the Northeast

Venerable Ajaan Khao spent the *vassa* of 1945-1946 in Mae Nong Harn, Sunsai district, Chiang Mai province. During the *vassa* he kindly gave a number of Dhamma talks to teach and instil faith into the people there. By that time, his *citta* had already gone free from the thick jungle and emerged into the land of boundless wide-open space. His *citta* had become a 'space *citta*' and his Dhamma had become 'space Dhamma', both of them interfused into one in complete fulfilment. Nothing ever came to obstruct and deceive him like it used to. He continued his normal daily activities for the sake of maintaining the body and the *khandhas* so that the Dhamma dwelling place (*vihāra-dhamma*) of the *citta* in this world (*diṭṭha-dhamma*) would remain convenient and comfortable.

After the *vassa* he reflected back on his life before he set out to search for Dhamma and for the Path, Fruition and *Nibbāna*, by way of the constant practice of *Dhutanga Kammaṭṭhāna*. His past often came back to remind him of the promise which he had made soon after he was ordained. He had determined then that he would leave in order to search for the Dhamma in order to attain the Path, Fruition and *Nibbāna* and nothing else. When all the people and *ajaans* opposed him and tried to stop him from going away, he then announced with complete sincerity that:

"After I have gone, if I have not experienced Dhamma —
which is the Path, Fruition and *Nibbāna* — fully in my heart,
I will not return to let you ridicule me as a failure to my face.
This is my firm resolve. I will return only if I have this Dhamma
as my guarantee. I would like all of you to understand now that
it will be a long time before I return to see you again. By then,
you may have forgotten what I just told you."

When he had fully thought about it, he came to a defi-
nite decision and said farewell to all his friends and relatives
who were attached to him and did not want him to go. But
necessity compelled him to make a break with them, following the law of change which is bound to bring about separation
between people, both while living and at death, so everyone
has to accept this natural principle.

With that past incident fresh in his mind, Ajaan Khao
asked Ajaan Waen Sujino to accompany him back to the north
eastern region (Isahn) to visit his home village and all his
friends and relatives who he had left twenty years ago. Should
he wait any longer, he was concerned that either he or they
might die before there was a chance to meet again. Also, were
he to go now, he would have a very good opportunity to visit
and pay his respects to Venerable Ajaan Mun Bhūridatta, who
at that time was spending the *vassa* in Nong Pheu Nanai village in the Pannananikon district of Sakon Nakhon province
— an area where many *Dhutanga Kammaṭṭhāna Bhikkhus* lived
and practised.

But Ajaan Waen said that he would not go back as long
as he had still not attained the level of *Arahant*, which was
the goal that he was fully intent on achieving. He felt that he
had to stay put and go on developing until he reached his goal.

Then he could leave Chiang Mai and go elsewhere if he wanted to. But if he did not want to go anywhere, he would go on living in Chiang Mai until he died. He told Ajaan Khao:

"As for you, if you have attained *Arahantship* it would be very good if you spread the Dhamma among the Bhikkhus and villagers — to that I give my full approval and blessing. But please don't bring out the *kilesas* and false Dhamma to spread about to other people, because the *kilesas* and false Dhamma are abundant everywhere where people live in this world. In fact, they are never lacking in the hearts of those living in the world nowadays. For that reason, the world is full of trouble and turbulence and unable to find calm and peace either in body or mind. Wherever we go we hear nothing but complaints that life is full of suffering and difficulty, full of hardships and deprivations. Even in the villages and towns where they reckon that they are experiencing progress and development, we still hear complaints about suffering and difficulty.

"So when you go to the northeastern region, please teach Dhamma that is correct and complete, not lacking in any way; Dhamma that is calming and peaceful, not complaining and agitated. This is what you should take to give to them, so that your relatives and friends will all be full of gratitude and joy that you have come to visit.

"At present I am still fighting against the false Dhamma which makes me intoxicated. I haven't yet sobered up. I'm intoxicated while sitting, standing, walking and lying down. When sitting in *samādhi*, I'm intoxicated; walking *caṅkama bhāvanā*, I'm intoxicated. The *kilesas* that lead me into careless intoxication are still not ready to get off my shoulders, my back, my neck and my heart. However I twist and turn about, the intoxicating *kilesas* continue to do their work, interfering with all my actions of body, speech and mind. I have no way of knowing when I will be able to cure these intoxicants.

"But please go to Isahn and teach them about *madanimmadano* — that Dhamma which causes intoxicants to abate; *vaṭṭupacchedo* — that Dhamma which cuts out the worldly *citta*; *taṅhākkhayo* — that Dhamma which destroys craving; *virāgo* — that Dhamma which is the end of *rāga*[1], the pleasure of excitement; *nirodho* — that Dhamma which quenches all the *kilesas*; *Nibbāna* — the final and complete destruction of all the *kilesas* and the relative world of appearance. Go and spread these *dhammas* about in the monasteries and villages. People will be very glad and show their appreciation to you who have been away for such a long time."

That's what Ajaan Waen told Ajaan Khao when he was about to return to Isahn. Ajaan Waen did not accompany him, for he wanted to develop his practice until he attained the state of *Arahant* first. He had to put off any travel plans until after he had reached the goal that his heart was set on. So, instead, Ajaan Khao asked Ajaan Chob and Ajaan Butra to accompany him. Then the three of them left Chiang Mai and began walking cross-country to Isahn, where they intended first to pay their respects to Venerable Ajaan Mun at Wat Baan Nong Pheu in the district of Nanai, Sakon Nakhon province. The night before they reached there they stopped to rest for the night. While Ajaan Khao was doing his meditation practice, he thought reverently of Venerable Ajaan Mun, reflecting in his heart how at that time Ajaan Mun was probably sitting in meditation and looking right into their hearts and minds, seeing everything quite clearly throughout. Ajaan Khao suspected that even before they had reached him, there was probably nothing within their hearts that Ajaan Mun had not found out with his super-knowing *ñāṇa*.

It was rather amazing that what he thought turned out to be true. For when they got there and met Venerable Ajaan Mun, he gave them an important talk on Dhamma, saying:

"Being afraid that other people will look into your heart and mind, rather than being concerned about looking into your own heart and mind to see what's there, is simply wasting your time dreaming and thinking externally while having no interest in thinking about going into your own body and mind. Where else can we who practise the way find the ability to be circumspect? Those who practise so as to know the basic principles of truth must look at themselves and their own hearts — the major cause of all problems — far more than looking at things outside themselves. They must also find a method of guarding themselves and their hearts by being careful and watchful in all postures and situations. They must use their mindfulness and wisdom to recollect and learn from their past experience, so they can think about and work out how to deal with each incident that they meet up with. They must not be careless and indifferent with anything in the sphere of the relative world of convention, which is nothing but the sphere of *dukkha*, the sphere of birth and death of all beings in the world."

After having rested and listened to Venerable Ajaan Mun's Dhamma, which gave them a feeling of uplift and joy, they saluted him and took their leave. They then went wandering in the vicinity of Ajaan Mun's forest monastery to find solitude, practising the way of *Kammaṭṭhāna* in places such as Baan Koke Manao and Baan Gut Baak in Gut Baak district, Sakon Nakhon province. They promoted their striving in Dhamma continuously in that area for several months, after which they all set off to go to Ajaan Khao's home village.

When they reached his home village where he was born and grew up, all the people there, including his relatives and friends, were very happy and elated to hear about his arrival. They asked him to have *mettā* for them by spending the next *vassa* period there. When he agreed, they built a hut for him to stay the *vassa* at Bor Chaneng — which was the name of his home village.

After the *vassa* period, Ajaan Khao said farewell to all his relatives and friends and returned to Sakon Nakhon province. There he went wandering in various districts where there were forests and hills which were suitable for practising the way of *Samaṇa-dhamma*, such as the foothills of Phu Pan and Phu Lek ranges in the district of Sawang Daen Din. He spent several *vassa* periods in that area: one year at Nong Luang village, another at Thum Ped, another at Wai Sanoi village and another at Chum Pon village, all of which are within the boundaries of the district of Sawang Daen Din, Sakon Nakhon province. He had a few Bhikkhus and novices with him, but not many, because he did not want a lot of people following him around. It would have been too disturbing and too difficult to find suitable places to stay and practice, as well as being difficult to gather food on *piṇḍapāta*. He preferred staying near small villages composed of not more than five, six or seven houses, as this provided the most suitable conditions for the way of *Samaṇa-dhamma* by avoiding the disturbances of a large crowd of Bhikkhus and novices constantly coming and going as he had found in the larger villages and monasteries he had seen.

AJAAN KHAO WAS SO ABSOLUTELY RESOLUTE and resourceful in striving that it would be hard to find anyone else to equal him. When it came to striving in the way of Dhamma, even in old age he still remained very skilled and resolute without weakening. When he walked *caṅkama*, he continued for five or six hours each time before taking a rest. Even the young Bhikkhus could not equal him. The striving of the wisest men is so very different from that of the rest of us, who tend to look forward more to the time when we can rest our heads on our pillows. As if pillows are more exalted than the Path, Fruition and *Nibbāna* – which, when one looks at it and thinks about it, should make us ashamed of how clever we are in those ways that are completely lacking in essential value.

Visions of Ajaan Mun

For several years Venerable Ajaan Khao spent the *vassa* period living in the hills alone, relying on two or three families of farmers to give him food when he went out on *piṇḍapāta* each day. For those who are ordained as Bhikkhus, this type of life provides the most happiness and peace of heart in the practice of Dhamma. Since there are no other burdens or duties

103

to trouble one, all one's time is filled with the effort to practise the way. One's time is always one's own; one's effort is one's own in every situation; and the *citta* with Dhamma is one's own in all that one does. There is nothing distracting to divide one's attention, causing it to deteriorate. A Bhikkhu who lives in the present, as if tonight is the only night left to him, is not concerned with how much longer he is going to live, or with other distractions, for what he is doing is of incomparably greater value than anything else.

Venerable Ajaan Khao said that when he spent the *vassa* period by himself in the hills along the borders of Sakon Nakhon and Kalasin provinces, he lived in a place three or four miles distant from the nearest village. Many wild animals roamed that district, including tigers, elephants, wild oxen, red bulls, wild boar, barking deer and various other kinds of deer. At night he used to hear these animals' calls echoing through the forest as they roamed in search of food, often coming close to where he was staying. Sometimes they came so close that he could almost make out what kind of animal it was. Seeing these animals made him feel joyful, with *mettā* and compassion for them.

It was soon after Venerable Ajaan Mun died that Ajaan Khao spent the *vassa* period in those hills. He said that when he practised *samādhi* meditation during that period, Ajaan Mun came to visit him regularly in his meditation to talk about Dhamma and give him 'friendly Dhamma advice' (*sammodaniya-dhamma*). When doing his routine duties in the vicinity of the cave where he stayed, or when arranging his few possessions, if he did anything improperly, Ajaan Mun would point it out to him in his *samādhi* meditation every time.

For that reason, it seemed as though he was living with Ajaan Mun for the whole of that *vassa* period.

Ajaan Mun came into his meditation and told him about the customs and traditions of *Dhutanga Bhikkhus* who are intent on attaining freedom. He emphasised that the various *dhutanga* observances should be maintained and done properly in the way that the Lord Buddha prescribed — they should not be altered. Then he talked about the *dhutanga* practices that he taught his disciples to follow while he was still alive, repeating what he said for emphasis thus:

"Throughout my life right up to the end I taught my disciples to observe those *dhutanga* practices which I knew about with certainty — without any doubt at all. So you should take them to heart and practise them with a full and complete commitment. You should never think that the *Sāsana* is the exclusive property of the Lord Buddha or any of his *Sāvaka* disciples. For, in fact, the *Sāsana* belongs to whoever cherishes it and is interested enough to practise the way, which includes everyone who aims to gain value from the *Sāsana*. The Lord Buddha and all the *Sāvakas* retained no part of the *Sāsana* which they gave fully and freely to the world. You should not think that the Lord and the *Sāvakas* would dispense both parts which were good as well as parts which were bad or tainted. Whether we practise the way rightly or wrongly is entirely up to each one of us — in no way does it depend on the Lord Buddha and the *Sāvakas*.

"You have come here with the specific purpose to practise the way. Whether you practise rightly or wrongly is also entirely up to you. So you must be very careful in what you do so as to live contentedly in the Dhamma of one who has seen the truth.

You will shortly become an *ācariya* with many followers, so you must set a good example to show what is right and seemly in order to be an exalted symbol of righteousness and truth and a blessing to all who follow after you — so that those who follow you will not be disappointed. Being an *ācariya* is a very important position, so you should examine what it means carefully. For if the *ācariya* himself goes wrong, he may also lead many others in the wrong direction. But if he does what is right, he can equally lead countless others in the right direction. You should therefore carefully examine all aspects of what it means to be an *ācariya* with many followers. Others will then have an unobstructed, smooth path to follow, which will not be false because you, as their *ācariya*, taught them wrongly.

"The word '*ācariya*' means one who trains and develops his behaviour, which is displayed externally in his actions and manners, in such a way that those who depend on him can hold him up as an example to be followed. His should not be the kind of behaviour that displays falsehood due to a lack of prior thought and consideration. The Lord Buddha, who we call the *Sāsadā* — the Great Teacher of the world — was not the *Sāsadā* only at those times when he was giving a talk on Dhamma to Buddhists who came to listen to him. He was the *Sāsadā* at all times, in every situation and position, whether reclining on his right side in the 'Lion posture', sitting, standing or walking about. Even when he was within a Buddhist monastery, the Lord would still be the *Sāsadā* in every action and every movement he made, never doing anything that was uncharacteristic of the *Sāsadā*. Therefore, anyone who has mindfulness and wisdom and an inclination towards critical assessment and contemplation can always take every movement and every gesture that the Lord made as a teaching and a moral example.

"You should not think that the Lord ever behaved in an unrestrained manner, like worldly people who like to adjust and change their behaviour depending on the people and circumstances that they come across. For they behave like this in one place and act like that in another — which is the characteristic behaviour of ghosts and *pretas*. There are both good people and bad people all over the world who do not have enough of a presence within them to hold on to as a firm, stable principle, so they cannot be a source of stability to others. Unlike worldly people, the Lord Buddha was the Great Teacher in everything he did right up to the day of final *Nibbāna*. Whatever action or characteristic he displayed, he was always the *Sāsadā*, never being deficient or incapable. So whoever holds to him as a 'refuge' — which means a basic principle or example of how one should act and behave — can do so at any time in whatever they are doing, by following his example, without any doubt as to whether the example of the Lord is suited to that occasion or not. This is why the title of the 'Great Teacher of the triple world system' — *Sāsadā* — is well suited to the Lord.

"When the Lord was about to enter *Parinibbāna*, he did so in the 'Lion posture'. He did not lie down carelessly, as though he had thrown away his limbs and body, afraid of death and repeating mantras and magical verses so that he would go to this or that realm of existence — which is the way of ordinary people everywhere in the world. But he died composed, in the 'Lion posture', and entered *Parinibbāna*. Meanwhile, his heart went through the process of 'entering *Nibbāna*' with unwavering courage and discipline — as though he were about to go on living in the world for a long time to come. Actually the Lord proclaimed that he was the Great Teacher in those final moments by entering the *Jhānas* and *Nirodha Samāpatti*[2] and then withdrawing from them when the right moment came to enter *Parinibbāna*, fully confirming his status as the Great Teacher without any remaining attachments to anything in the three worlds of existence. In this way, from the moment of his enlightenment to the time of his *Parinibbāna*, the Lord Buddha made his behaviour an example for the whole world to follow. He never reduced his standards of behaviour below those required of the Great Teacher, behaving in any way like ordinary, worldly people. He dutifully maintained his position of perfection right to the end.

"You should therefore take up the example of the *Sāsadā* and put it into practice. Although you will not be able to match the perfection of the Lord in all respects, your behaviour will still be in the category of one who follows the word of the Teacher — not drifting uncontrolled like a boat adrift in a storm in the middle of the ocean that has not put out its anchor. The practice of a monk who has no correct, firmly-established principles within him is likely to lack any real purpose that enables him to determine whether he will reach a safe shore, or whether he will meet various dangers ahead. He is like a boat without a rudder that is not likely to be able to take him where he wants to go. Consequently, he is bound to drift with the ocean currents, which can easily lead him into great danger.

"The basic principles of Dhamma and *Vinaya*, such as the *dhutanga* observances, are the 'rudders' of the practice, which lead it to a safe goal. Because of that, you should take hold of them and grasp them firmly. You must not waver or vacillate, which would lead those who follow you to follow a bad example and go wrong accordingly. The *dhutanga* observances are the practices which proceed directly towards the goal – no other practice can equal them in this. If those who practice the *dhutangas* use mindfulness, wisdom, faith and effort in their striving, then that Dhamma which they are hoping to attain should be well within the scope of these practices. As they have been handed down to us by the Lord Buddha, it is quite certain that they are capable of leading us to success without any doubts or obstacles being able to prevent us. The *dhutanga* observances are the only way that can lead us beyond *dukkha*. There is no other way, so you should not feel uncertain or doubtful. The *dhutangas* are the place where all the methods of practice converge and lead into the process of quenching all *dukkha*.

"Those Bhikkhus who prefer the *dhutanga* observances as their mode of development are those who are faithful to the teaching of the Lord Buddha, who was the First Teacher. Those Bhikkhus who have taken up the *dhutanga* observances as their path of practice are those who have proper restraint, with the Buddha as their refuge in all situations. Wherever they go or stay they have Dhamma to help protect them as a substitute for the *Sāsadā*. They are not lonely, aimless or unstable, for the heart's principle is the principle of Dhamma, and the principle of Dhamma is identical with the heart. Breathing in and breathing out is Dhamma, which is intimately blended into a single unity with the heart. Such people are always living with Dhamma, never being disturbed or biased.

"For yourself, it is true that you do not have anything to worry about in terms of Dhamma. But many people will associate with you in the future, so you must have concern for all those who follow you, both fellow monks and lay people as well, so that they may feel confident that the practices they have picked up from you are the correct way to make progress without mistake."

This was how Venerable Ajaan Mun taught Ajaan Khao as he sat in meditation. If he slept over the time for him to wake, even just a little, Ajaan Mun would come and point it out to him, saying:

"Don't trust yourself more than Dhamma, for 'yourself' is really just the round of *saṁsāra*. The elements of the body and the *khandhas* are results that have come from the round of *saṁsāra*, right from the beginning. You should only give way to the *khandhas* to the extent that is necessary — but you must not give way to them more than you have to. Doing so goes against the basic nature of a Bhikkhu who is never complacent. For those who are truly wise, lying down to sleep is only for the purpose of giving a temporary relief to the physical body. They do not expect to gain pleasure or contentment from resting to relieve the tiredness and weakness of the physical *khandha*. The Bhikkhu who lies down as a Bhikkhu should, must be careful to remind himself of the time to get up — like a deer that lies down to rest while roaming for food must be more mindful and careful than normal. To 'lie down properly'[3] means to carefully set up mindfulness before going to sleep, making the resolve to get up at a predetermined time — not lying down in the manner of one who auctions off his goods as though they are worthless, letting the customer give whatever he feels like giving for them. The Bhikkhu who lies down and lets his body go however it will is not a Son of the *Sākya* – a Buddhist who guards the religion, promoting it in himself and in others – but a Bhikkhu who auctions everything off arbitrarily, letting the buyer fix the price.

"To lie down properly in the manner of a Bhikkhu who is endowed with *sīla* and Dhamma as religious duties, a Bhikkhu must have a regular procedure that he follows before going to sleep. This habit makes him careful and self-possessed when he lies down to sleep. As soon as he wakes he must get up quickly, and not linger in bed – which is the way of a lazy person who tends to get up late, and who dies immersed in careless indifference, never waking enough to become aware of himself. Lying down like this is the way of a worthless animal, or of a lazy person who destroys whatever value he has and is unable to rise up and improve himself. Since such behaviour is not the way of the *Sāsana*, it should not be encouraged; or else it will become a 'parasite creeper' growing within the *Sāsana* and within the whole company of *Dhutanga Bhikkhus*. It can easily destroy you, just as a 'parasite creeper' destroys the tree on which it depends. You should think about and compare the two concepts of 'lying down properly' and 'lying down in the usual way'. Compare them and search out where they differ, for the 'lying down properly' of a Son of the *Sākya* is very different from the ordinary 'lying down' of people and animals everywhere. Therefore, the Sons of the *Sākya* feel that to 'lie down properly' each and every time they rest has a special significance which remains close to their hearts all the time. This is appropriate for one who maintains mindfulness and who has the wisdom to use thought and contemplation in everything that he does. Not merely thinking any old way, or speaking any old way, or acting any old way; not merely lying down, waking up, eating, standing, walking or sitting down any old way. All such negligent behaviour fails to live up to the standard of someone who has the status of a Son of the *Sākya*, who should never act in those ways.

"It is generally understood by people that after the Lord Buddha and each of the *Sāvaka Arahants* had entered final *Nibbāna*, they disappeared into oblivion and no longer had any meaning or relationship to the rest of us. But the Dhamma, which is the basic causal condition that teaches us to practise in the present, is this not the Dhamma of the one who dug deep, searched and brought it up for the world to see and to follow in practice? And the whole body of this Dhamma, how did it remain, and why did it not go into oblivion also? The fact is that both the 'Buddha' and 'Sangha' are the pure heart that has naturally transcended the limits of both death and annihilation. How could the pure *citta* die, be consigned to oblivion or become meaningless when its very nature does not accord with relative convention *(sammuti)*? When its nature no longer accords with relative convention, it is not subject to dying, or to being annihilated, or becoming meaningless. Thus, Buddha is Buddha in its own right; Dhamma is Dhamma in its own right; and Sangha is Sangha in its own right; and they are not shaken or influenced by any of the concepts of the relative world of conventions, which use their authority to create harmful ideas and attitudes within us. So, the whole time that we practise 'Dhamma which accords with Dhamma[4]' within the heart, it is like coming face to face with the Lord Buddha, the Dhamma and the Sangha at that time. When we know

Buddha, Dhamma and Sangha by natural principles, that knowing must arise in the heart, which is the most suitable dwelling place for Dhamma — no other vessel is more appropriate to it."

This is an example of the teaching with which Venerable Ajaan Mun admonished Ajaan Khao in his *samādhi* meditation practice when he saw that he had erred in some way; for instance, when he practised the *dhutanga* observances incorrectly or not strictly enough, or when he woke from sleep at the wrong time.

In truth, Ajaan Mun did not admonish him because he was convinced that he had done something wrong. Rather, he admonished him because he could see that in the future Ajaan Khao would be associated with many Bhikkhus and large numbers of lay people. For that reason, he often advised and admonished him so that he would become fully conscious of the strict ways of practising a monk's duties. Then he would be able to pass them on to all the other Bhikkhus and novices who come to live in dependence on him. And they in turn would gain something worthwhile to take away with them, just as Ajaan Mun's disciples had always done.

Venerable Ajaan Mun also taught him that all his possessions, such as the bowl, kettle, robes and other things that he used in his dwelling, should be neatly put away in their proper place. This also included such things as the rags for wiping his feet. Seeing that any of them were not clean enough, he should wash them before putting them to further use. After use, everything should be neatly put away, and not just left lying about all over the place. On any day that Ajaan Khao became so absorbed in other affairs that intruded into his life that he became forgetful or careless, a vision of Ajaan Mun would come to him in the middle of the night while he was practising *samādhi* meditation, admonishing him and pointing out the way of Dhamma to him.

HE STAYED ALONE IN THAT CAVE for the whole of the *vassa* period. At night he was frequently visited by Venerable Ajaan Mun who appeared in his meditation practice as a *nimitta*[5]. Sometimes sitting in meditation in the middle of the day when it was very quiet, he also saw Ajaan Mun come to visit him in the same way as he did at night. He said that it was very pleasurable for him to be able to ask Ajaan Mun all sorts of questions to make his understanding quite clear. Ajaan Mun was very proficient at answering questions with great skill and dexterity. He made the answer so clear as to remove all doubt and uncertainty every time. With some questions, Ajaan Khao had only a feeling of uncertainty, but he did not actually think of asking about it. Nonetheless, at night when he did his meditation practice, Ajaan Mun would come and bring up that question for discussion, as though he had just asked him about it. Ajaan Khao said it was truly strange and wonderful – but he could not tell anyone else because they would probably pass him off as a 'mad *kammaṭṭhāna* monk'. Mostly, the Dhamma for curing the various *kilesas* arose from *nimittas* in *samādhi* meditation, such as those of Ajaan Mun coming frequently to admonish him, to show him the right way and to give him Dhamma teaching. This promoted his mindfulness and wisdom, making him think and consider carefully, leaving no room for carelessness.

In marked contrast to all other places he had lived, the *vassa* period that he spent in that cave in the desolate jungle enabled him to develop various skilful methods, both internally and externally, which arose very frequently at all times of the day and night. Ajaan Khao was someone who lived in the present[6] with joy in Dhamma in all postures and situations. Whether standing, walking, sitting or lying down, he was filled with the bliss of Dhamma in the midst of the peaceful Dhamma that was the original foundation of his pure *citta*, which was completely pure amidst the various kinds of phenomena that made contact with the heart, displaying their meanings in various ways. The bliss of Dhamma refreshed his body and mind, making them joyful; like a tree being cared for and supplied with fertiliser and water, and growing in a suitable climate and environment, which always keeps it fresh and moist both in the trunk and throughout all its branches, twigs, leaves and fruit.

Ajaan Khao said that when the *citta* remains only in the present with the calm and peace of Dhamma, then regardless of how much we get involved in things that are confusing and distracting, we still have nothing but happiness while living in the world of involvement with our own *khandhas*. We need not struggle to find happiness and contentment in other places or other realms — which is merely creating images to deceive ourselves, causing us to develop a strong craving *(taṅhā)* which promotes the Cause of *Dukkha* that becomes the fuel which burns us and causes us so much misery. The happiness that is known and experienced in the heart is a happiness which is already sufficient and complete. Then, this entire world and all other worlds, however many there may be in the universe of *saṁsāra*, appear not to exist. That which does exist, and which is quite clear and apparent, is the *citta* with Dhamma which seems to cover the whole universe — though it is impossible to explain this or compare it to anything, because there are no characteristics or data by which one can classify it. The *citta* that possesses the Ultimate Dhamma — *Acchariya Dhamma* — does not exist within the realms of convention, so there is no basis for making any comparisons or suppositions.

Living with Tigers

After the end of that *vassa* period, some faithful lay supporters from Sawang Daen Din in Sakon Nakhon province travelled to the cave to invite him to return with them and kindly be their teacher. So he was obliged to leave the place where he had been staying, even though he longed to remain there as he had not thought of going elsewhere for a long time. Having taught the villagers for some time, he took leave of them and went wandering wherever he felt like going in the manner of *Dhutanga Kammaṭṭhāna Bhikkhu*. Sometimes he crossed the Mekong River into Laos, where he stayed on the banks of the river. Later he crossed back into Thailand and continued wandering and practising the way in Dong Mor Tong, a mountainous area covered with thick jungle which straddles the districts of Bung Kan and Phon Phisai. In that area were many good places suitable for practising the way. There were also some newly established villages made up of only a few houses. The people in those villages invited him to spend the *vassa* there for their benefit. As it was a place that suited his temperament, he agreed to stay there for the *vassa* period.

While he was staying and practising Dhamma in the hills of the Phon Phisai district, he was fascinated and glad at heart to see all the different kinds of animals living there, for whom he had much *mettā*. The animals he saw included: wild fowl, pheasant, all sorts of birds like hornbill and peacock, as well as animals like the palm civet, barking deer, wild boar, ordinary deer, monkeys of various kinds, gibbon apes, wild dogs, tigers, leopards, elephants, wild oxen and red bulls. He saw far more of each of those species there than he had seen anywhere else. There were herds of them roaming everywhere. Day and night, he could hear their cries echoing loudly through the forest, each group according to its own natural rhythm.

Some days when he went out walking for *piṇḍapāta*, he saw a large tiger walking most gracefully in the forest ahead of him. It was quite close to him, walking fearlessly, proud and dignified as is its nature. When there was a clearing in the forest ahead of him, it was beautiful to see the way it walked. The first time he saw the tiger, it glanced at him just momentarily and went on walking without looking back at him again, as though it was not in the least afraid of him. But inwardly it was probably careful and watchful, which is in character for an animal that has good mindfulness and is inherently cautious — it does not easily relax and make a mistake. As for Ajaan Khao, he had no thought of fear for the tiger because he had seen them before on many occasions. He had heard them growling and roaring so often while staying in the forests that he travelled through, where it was quite normal for such animals to live, that he was quite accustomed to them and had no fear of them.

One evening during the *vassa* as he sat teaching the way of *Kammaṭṭhāna* to the several Bhikkhus staying with him, he heard three large striped tigers roaring in the distance, each one in a different direction. After a while he heard them growling threateningly and fighting with each other. Then they went completely quiet. Later he heard them growling and fighting close by. In the beginning, he heard them playing and fighting outside the area where the Bhikkhus were staying. When they subsequently went quiet, he thought they had moved on somewhere else. But that wasn't the case, for at about 9 p.m. they approached the small meeting hall (*sālā*) where the Bhikkhus were sitting in *samādhi*, listening to the Dhamma teaching, and crawled into the space under the floor. The floor of the *sālā* was raised just over one meter above the ground, and the sound of these tigers roaring and growling and fighting there together was so disrupting that Ajaan Khao had to shout at them, saying:

"Hey! My three friends! Don't make such a noise! The Bhikkhus are listening to a talk on Dhamma. Doing evil like this could land you in hell — don't say I didn't warn you! This is not the right place to cause a commotion, so you should all go away and roar elsewhere. This is a monastery for Bhikkhus who like to develop calm — unlike you — so go roar to your heart's content somewhere else where nobody will interfere with you. Here the Bhikkhus practise the way of Dhamma and they do not give you permission to make a lot of noise and disturbance."

As soon as they heard Ajaan Khao shouting at them, they went quiet and still for a short while, but he could still hear them, as if they were whispering to each other quietly under the *sālā*, saying: "We better not make much noise, the Bhikkhus are annoyed and shouting at us, so we must talk quietly or else it will be bad and we may soon end up with sores on our heads." But after a while they again started growling and playfully fighting each other. They did not seem to want to go elsewhere, as Ajaan Khao had told them to do. It seemed as though they had all agreed that under the floor of the *sālā* was the place for them to play and have fun from dusk until midnight, when they finally went away. Meanwhile, after Ajaan Khao had finished his teaching, the Bhikkhus remained sitting there doing their *samādhi* practice while the three large tigers played, fighting and growling and making a lot of noise under the *sālā*, until they went back into the forest at midnight. Only then did the Bhikkhus return to their individual dwelling places.

This incident was most strange and unusual. For many years Ajaan Khao had wandered in the way of *Kammaṭṭhāna* through forested areas in many different parts of the country, but he had never before seen or heard of tigers coming so close to people in a friendly manner, as if they had been close friends of the Bhikkhus for a long time. Normally, tigers are instinctively afraid of people, even though they are so powerful that they make people more afraid of them than almost any other animal. In general, tigers are more afraid of people than people are of tigers, so they avoid people and keep away from them. Yet these three tigers were not only unafraid of people, they even went to the extent of taking possession of the space under the floor of the small *sālā* to play and have fun together while

119

a lot of Bhikkhus were gathered right above them. Apparently, they were not in the least afraid of the Bhikkhus, who were human beings just like people everywhere. This was quite remarkable, for such animals know nothing of morality, which all people know about, yet their behaviour in coming into close proximity to the Bhikkhus made it look almost as though they had a good understanding of morality, which they put into practice in the way that people do. They never once displayed any menacing behaviour towards the Bhikkhus, although they probably did so towards each other in the knowledge that they all understood what their intentions were.

Even though it took place a long time ago, I felt as if my hair was standing on end with fear while I listened to Ajaan Khao telling me about this incident — which was rather silly. Foolish, silly people are like that: even if the *ajaans* tell them stories which have a moral lessons of Dhamma buried in them, foolish and incompetent people are unlikely to listen for the purpose of extracting the moral principles from it. Instead, they show their lack of intelligence by focusing just on the story-line itself. Like myself, who showed fear shamelessly in front of Ajaan Khao while listening to his story. In addition, in writing this book I am also displaying my timidity for those who read it to laugh at me — which is bad enough! So, having read this, please be careful not to let this kind of story penetrate your heart and haunt it, or else many of you are likely to become timid and silly people also!

Most of the Bhikkhus who sat in meditation listening to Ajaan Khao teaching that night were stirred up and frightened, both while they sat there and after they left the *sālā*. Their eyes and ears were wide open when they heard the 'three great teachers' crawl under the *sālā* to help Ajaan Khao teach them a lesson. When their sense of contentment was confronted by their fear of tigers, the Bhikkhus sitting there were scared stiff. They did not dare to let their *cittas* wander out freely, for fear that those three teachers might decide to jump up onto the floor of the *sālā* and give them 'instructions'.

Actually the behaviour of the three tigers was praiseworthy in that they did nothing unreasonably excessive or violent, such as leaping onto the floor of the *sālā*. They knew what their basic situation in life was, and to some extent, what that of the Bhikkhus was, and they did not go beyond what was proper for them in their situation. Their activities were all gentle and harmonious — then they simply went away. After that they never returned, although the district where the Bhikkhus were staying was a place where tigers and all sorts of other animals roamed freely. There was never a night without some tigers wandering about the area, because it was a most suitable living environment for all sorts of wild animals. That whole mountainous area was covered with thick forest so extensive that it would take a person many days to walk all the way through it. Many varieties of wild animals lived there in large numbers. There were many large herds of elephants and packs of wild boar — and they were not very afraid of people.

Many skilful teaching methods occurred to Ajaan Khao during the year that he lived in that mountainous region. He often had to warn the other Bhikkhus who were with him not to be careless in maintaining the *dhutanga* observances. He reminded them that they were living in an environment which made it necessary for them to be careful of many things. They had to depend on the *dhutanga* observances as their lifeline, and fully entrust their lives to the Dhamma and *Vinaya*. In that way, they could live happily without being scared and apprehensive of things in the natural environment that might otherwise have startled them.

Ajaan Khao and his disciples ate very little food — just enough to act as a 'medicine' to support their bodies and keep them going from day to day. The village they depended on for food was newly-built and had yet to become firmly-established, so they had very few lay supporters. But, because they had pledged themselves to Dhamma, those Bhikkhus intended to train themselves to put up with difficulties for the sake of the Dhamma of inner peace. So they were not much concerned about their living conditions, or about how much food they got on *piṇḍapāta*, for such concerns could easily become obstacles in the way of what they were trying to accomplish. As for medical remedies, they considered putting up with pain and fighting sickness by striving hard in *samādhi bhāvanā* to be the most effective cures. They considered the animals that lived in the surrounding forest to be their friends and took them as examples; for they never had any medicines available to them; nor were they born in a hospital with doctors and midwives to aid them. Yet there they were! Animals of all sorts, quite able to keep their family lines going, and in large numbers too! And they never showed any grief or discouragement at their lack of medical attention from doctors, nurses and all sorts of medicines and medical devices.

Bhikkhus are human beings. They are Sons of the *Sākya* — the Great Teacher — whose name resounds throughout the three worlds as one who learned everything there was to know in the 'books' of the three levels of existence by using his endurance, effort, wisdom, skill and ability to the fullest. Never was he caught at a loss, unable to find a way out; nor was he ever weak and lazy and inclined to give up. If Bhikkhus retreat, shedding tears just because of the suffering and hardships of the aches and pains experienced in sickness, which are natural conditions of the *khandhas* anyway, they are bound to lose out and go 'bankrupt', and so will not be able to guide themselves or the religion properly. Unless they are courageous and firm in putting up with natural conditions — living and experiencing them all with mindfulness and wisdom to assess and know each and every event that they come into contact with — there is no way to save themselves and escape to a lasting safe haven.

When the *citta* has been trained in the right way, it will find joy in Dhamma. It will gladly guide a Bhikkhu to the right methods for attaining the Path and Fruition without changing course or creating obstacles to cause him more trouble. The practice of the way will then steadily progress without slipping backwards, so he won't feel disheartened because he has no inner refuge. He will have the 'heart with Dhamma' to cleanse, to soothe and to protect him, causing him to feel peaceful and secure. Then wherever he goes or wherever he stays, he is inherently content — *sugato* — in the manner of true disciples of the *Tathāgata*, without any signs of impoverishment in his heart. Those *Dhutanga Kammaṭṭhāna Bhikkhus* who are intent on Dhamma go about and live their lives like this. They can stay anywhere and go anywhere, for they are prepared to put up with hardship and hunger while remaining contented and free from anxiety, with Dhamma as the object of attachment (*ārammaṇa*) of their hearts.

It may be difficult for the reader to accept some of the things that happen in connection with the forest animals that like to come and live close to Bhikkhus. So, to begin with, it may be better to consider domestic animals which people like to look after with *mettā* in their homes, and animals that seek sanctuary in the monasteries. The number of animals such as dogs and birds that want to live in monasteries increases every day, until there is hardly any room left for the dogs — or trees left for the birds.

Having thought about the domestic animals with which we are all familiar, we can go on to consider the various kinds of wild animals that tend to hang around the forest locales or the monasteries where *Dhutanga Bhikkhus* tend to stay. I have already written about such animals in the books "Biography of Venerable Ajaan Mun" and "Paṭipada", where many incidents are related of animals coming to live near the Bhikkhus. All of which are experiences that I know to be true.

From the viewpoint of Dhamma, these stories are quite interesting, for Dhamma is the principle of nature that gives peace and happiness. And Dhamma treats all species equally, regardless of whether or not they actually understand what Dhamma is. There is something which manifests in the experience of all beings that they are happy to accept, something which no one dislikes. That something is the natural Dhamma which manifests as calm and happiness, as peace, as trust and confidence, as goodwill, as *mettā*, as affection and compassion, and as tolerance in which others are free to come or go as they will, without fear or danger. These are some of the things that flow from Dhamma. Animals of all kinds like it and readily accept it without any need to attend school to be taught about it. The *citta* is far more compatible with the out-flow of Dhamma than it is with the possession of external titles, rank or authority, which are like ornaments that increase one's self-importance, but can easily dissolve away and disappear depending on circumstances which are fickle and uncertain. Therefore, although animals don't really know what Dhamma is, they will tend to search on their own for those things which they naturally like and can readily accept; for instance, stray dogs staying in a monastery or wild animals living close by *Dhutanga Bhikkhus*. Animals instinctively understand that Dhamma — which means peace and security — is to be found in those places, so they search for it in their own way. Even people who've never shown any interest in Dhamma know those places which are secure and safe, and they enjoy relaxing and having fun in such places. They realise that it would not be safe to act like that in other places. This has been the case from ancient times to the present day.

This explanation should be sufficient to understand how Dhamma, and the places where people live and practise Dhamma, make animals and people everywhere feel confident and free from danger. So they tend to relax and dispense with their usual caution. There are even some who go so far as to forget themselves completely, without stopping to consider how other people feel about it, or whether their behaviour is appropriate for the religion, which is the treasure of the whole country. Even people like that know the difference between good and evil. They know the difference between good people and bad people, between good animals and bad animals, in the same way that people everywhere do. So they should think of others and how much they cherish their treasure, and they

125

should refrain from letting go of all restraint. Limits and bounds exist within which people and animals should remain, each in its own sphere. They should not mix up their modes of behaviour until they are all behaving in the same way, so one cannot tell which is which.

VENERABLE AJAAN KHAO had always liked wandering about the countryside searching for secluded places, so he frequently moved from one place to another. Even when staying in one locale, he liked to wander *dhutanga* through the surrounding forests and hills, frequently changing the place where he did his meditation. For example, he used a certain location as his base, but in the morning he would walk off somewhere else to do his practice. Then in the afternoon he would go to another place, and at night he would wander off to yet another place — all in the vicinity of his base. He also used to change the direction he went in, sometimes going far and sometimes close by. At times, he would change to another cave, moving from the cave which was his base, or he would go up to a rocky outcrop at the top of the mountain, returning to his base dwelling only late at night.

During the period when he was engaged in a fierce struggle with his defilements *(kilesas)*, he preferred this style of practice because he found that when he changed his situation constantly, wisdom would arise all the time. Then none of the defilements were able to get a grip on him, because they were constantly up against the skilful means of mindfulness and wisdom which beat them into a corner, trapping them so that they could be forced out and got rid of time after time. If he stayed always in one place, he would become accustomed to his surroundings and complacency would set in. But the *kilesas* would not become complacent. They would keep increasing regardless of what he was accustomed to. So he had to change about, altering his methods and his environment very frequently, in order to keep up with the deceptive tricks of the *kilesas*. For once they established themselves, they would accumulate and fight against him incessantly without ever taking time off for rest. If there was any respite from them, it was only in deep dreamless sleep; otherwise they were working all the time. Because of this, if he relaxed or weakened his efforts while striving to develop himself, putting off doing the practice and letting time slip by, it encouraged the ever-diligent *kilesas* to laugh at him. By changing locations and methods of practice very frequently, he could have some success in defeating the *kilesas*, which had no chance to feel satisfied that they were the sole master in charge.

His reasoning was most intriguing, and his practice was an excellent example for those who refuse to let the *kilesas* rise up and walk all over them due to an easygoing over-confidence that ruins every move that the *citta* makes.

VENERABLE AJAAN KHAO liked to wander in the districts of Phu Singh, Phu Wua, Phu Lanka, Dong Mor Tong; and in the districts of Ampher Seka and Ampher Phon Phisai in Nong Khai province; as well as Amphur Ban Phaeng in Nakhon Phanom province. These areas had plenty of mountains, such as Phu Singh, Phu Wua and Phu Lanka, which were all places suitable for the practice and development of Dhamma. But they were far away from villages — too far to go *piṇḍapāta* — so it was necessary to have people take turns bringing him food. All these places were full of wild animals of all sorts, including tigers, elephants, wild gaur and red oxen, among many others. In the afternoon and evening he could hear their calls and roars echoing throughout the forest. Anyone who had not truly overcome death would find it difficult to stay there, because there were many tigers in those places, far more than in other regions, and they were not afraid of people.

Some nights as he walked in meditation, one of the tigers would creep up and crouch down to watch him walking, without any fear of him at all. But it never harmed him. It may have simply wondered what he was up to, so it crept close to sniff and have a look. As soon as Ajaan Khao heard an unusual sound that made him suspicious, he would shine his flashlight there, only to see a great tiger leap away, sometimes very close in front of him. Even after that he was able to go on walking *caṅkama*, doing his meditation without any fear that the tiger might return to jump on him, maul him and eat him. His faith in Dhamma was stronger than his fear of the tiger, so he was able to persist and keep on doing his practice.

Sometimes in the evening he would climb up the hillside, from where he could see large herds of elephants going for a walk along a large area of rocky outcrops that stretched for miles. As the rocky area was not covered by forest, he could quite clearly see both large and small elephants going out to search for food. While watching those elephant herds having fun teasing each other and playing together, he became quite happily absorbed until the evening was late and it got too dark to see. It seems they liked to tease each other and play together in the same way as people do.

When Ajaan Khao lived in the forests and the mountains, he got the local villagers to lay out three different paths for walking meditation. He walked caṅkama on these three paths at three different times each day.

In the early evening, he began walking meditation on the path reserved for Sangha Pūjā.

Path Three

Sangha Pūjā

Cave of the Midday Drum

Beginning in early 1958, Venerable Ajaan Khao left Wat Pa Kaew Chumpon in the Sawang Daen Din district of Sakon Nakhon province, where he had stayed for several years, in order to wander in solitude. When he reached Udon Thani province, he wandered until he came to Wat Thum Klong Pain in the district of Nong Bua Lamphu. At that time, the whole area was covered in thick jungle. He saw that the place suited his disposition; he felt that he could stay there conveniently and practise the way of the *Samaṇa-dhamma*. So he settled down and remained there continually until the end of his life.

In regard to the name 'Thum Klong Pain': a long time ago, before it became a monastery, in Thum Klong Pain (lit. Cave of the Midday Drum), there used to hang a very large drum[1] which was struck to announce the noon hour to people over a very large area in that district. As to where it came from and who put it there, nobody seems to know anything about its origin. It had probably been there a long time — maybe hundreds of years — before it decayed and broke into many pieces on its own, without anyone doing any damage to it. Hunters who searched for game in the area sometimes rested in that cave.

They used to gather some of the bits of wood from the drum that were scattered about to make a fire to cook their meal and boil water. So the villagers who lived nearby gave the cave the name: Thum Klong Pain. Later on, *Dhutanga Kammaṭṭhāna Bhikkhus* often stayed in this cave while practising the way of Dhamma until it virtually became a Wat, for a Wat just means a place where Bhikkhus stay. So it came to be called Wat Thum Klong Pain, and it still has this name.

Originally there were a large number of Buddha images (*Buddha Rūpa*) in Thum Klong Pain, of many kinds and many different sizes. There were both those hidden out of sight, as well as those placed in full view of everyone. People have placed *Buddha Rūpas* in this cave since ancient times, and over the centuries they accumulated until there were a very large number, so many they were almost uncountable. There were many *Buddha Rūpas* made of gold, silver, 'nāga metal' (gold, copper alloy) and bronze. However, long ago the religion of *Māra* (the evil one) came and took the lot, leaving none behind. All that's left are the ordinary *Buddha Rūpas* made of stone or plaster which are there now.

IT IS IMPORTANT THAT WE BUDDHISTS understand clearly that the monastery is an important place in the sphere of Buddhism. Normally, devout Buddhists cannot go into a monastery, or travel past one, without having good and exalted thoughts arising within their hearts. This is because 'the monastery' has always been a sacred place since the remote past, regardless of whether it is in the village or in the forest. The monastery is the place where the *citta* and all sacred things come together, a place where countless Buddhists have been able to realise their highest aspirations. The monastery may be run down and in a state of disrepair, or well appointed and beautiful, but in the hearts of all those people who have faith in Buddhism there will be a constant attitude of respect and homage for it.

For these reasons, whenever Buddhists go into a Buddhist monastery, for whatever purpose, they should be self-restrained, making sure that their behaviour is sufficiently modest and suitable. This also includes the clothes that people wear: they should be very careful to make sure that their dress conforms to their status as 'children of the Buddha' who are going into a place which is highly sacred, a place which has been glorified by the Lord Buddha, the Great Teacher of the three worlds.

This dress code is especially important in the forest monastery, where Bhikkhus tend to be a bit like monkeys that have never had the opportunity to see and admire the material progress and the latest cultural developments that have taken place in cities and towns. When they see people coming to the monastery wearing some of the latest fashions, they feel it's rather frightening and peculiar. It's almost enough to make them dizzy and feverish — probably because they get a sudden fright from seeing something they have never seen before. They are so used to living in the forest that they have become part of it; and in such an environment it is not easy to imagine such things. So when they suddenly see strange things which depart from the way of Dhamma, an unusual change takes place in their minds and they feel profoundly dismayed.

Most forest *Dhutanga Bhikkhus* say they have a similar kind of reaction; and we should sympathise with them. If someone were to explain to them about the material and cultural

135

developments taking place in the towns and cities nowadays — telling them that progress is taking place with equal swiftness both nationally and internationally, both within towns and in the countryside, within village monasteries and in the forest ones — they would most likely not believe it. In fact, they would probably just feel disgusted, apprehensive and dismayed about the whole matter. In the end, the person relating these developments would be at his wits' end, unable to relieve the forest Bhikkhus' apprehensions. He would be left feeling sorry for those primitive forest monks who live so far from the progress of modern civilization.

THE MONASTERY WHERE Venerable Ajaan Khao lived is located in the forests and the hills. The natural environment is well suited to the development of meditation and the practice of Dhamma, for it is full of boulders, cliffs and forests with pleasant, shady trees. Ajaan Khao always tried to avoid the excesses of modern society that I've already mentioned. If you were to say that he was uncivilised like most of the *Dhutanga Bhikkhus*, then you would not be wrong. His Dhamma virtue was exceptionally high — he was entirely beyond reproach, in my opinion. But presumably he retained the habit of being very watchful and afraid of dangers in the forest; for even though his Dhamma virtue was at the highest level, he would not have been able to give up all his latent habitual tendencies. This accords with the Dhamma saying of the Lord, which says: the *Sāvakas* cannot entirely give up their original habitual tendencies, for only the Lord Buddha was able to get rid of his latent habitual tendencies *(nissāya)* completely, along with his good characteristics *(vāsanā)*.

Whenever crowds of people came to his monastery causing a lot of unwanted disturbance, Ajaan Khao would disappear quickly into the forest and hide in a crevice between the rocks until all had quieted down. Only in the evening, or after night had fallen, did he return to his residence. When asked why he slipped away like that, he answered:

"My Dhamma is not sufficient to withstand the strong flowing current of the world, so I have to run away and hide. If I didn't do this, but stayed and put up with it, my Dhamma would surely break up and disintegrate. So I must go where I can look after myself. Though I don't have the ability to help these people, I should at least think about helping myself."

To the best of my knowledge, Ajaan Khao had a lot of *mettā* and generally gave a great deal of help to other people. But on those occasions when he escaped and went into hiding, it was probably because it was beyond his ability to put up with them — as he himself has said. Whether they intend to or not, the majority of people who come to the monastery tend to continually destroy the peaceful atmosphere there. Very few actually try to uphold and maintain *Sīla-dhamma* and virtue at the monastery. In the end, the monks are bound to become frustrated when they cannot put up with the added burden.

Generally speaking, lay people tend to watch the Bhikkhus much more than they observe themselves. When they go to a place where they should have faith and pay respect, their manners and their speech tend to be quite offensive to the eyes and ears. Such behaviour is thought-provoking for those who like to observe how careless and lacking in restraint people can be, without any interest in themselves or how they might appear to other people. This is what's so frustrating.

Master Hunter Boon Nah

It is the normal practice in Thailand, and other Buddhist countries, for people to pay respect and perform *pūjā* before a *Buddha Rūpa*. Nobody looks at it as in any way being an evil practice that brings harm or suffering to people. So regardless of whether a person has a good nature or an evil nature, when he comes across a *Buddha Rūpa*, his mind tends to become compliant and respectful. He instinctively salutes it with reverence, never looking upon it as an enemy in any way. The *Buddha Rūpas* in Thum Klong Pain also acted in this way. Whenever hunters spent the night resting in this cave, they would pay obeisance to the *Buddha Rūpas* and ask forgiveness for the bad things they had done.

But once, a rather strange and peculiar hunter came to rest in the cave. He made a prayer, asking the *Buddha Rūpas* to help bring him animals whose meat he could take as food, such as barking deer and ordinary deer. "May they be unsteady, their eyes dimmed and their senses dulled, walking clumsily, sluggishly, like an animal that is almost dead near the hunter who is already prepared and waiting so that he can shoot it and then carry it away without further concern."

This strange hunter did not think and act in the same way as ordinary people at all. His name was Master Hunter Boon Nah, a name his father and mother gave him on the day that he was born (but in fact, his name should have been changed to accord with what he did that day, when the name Master Baap Nah would be more suitable).[2] That day he went searching and hunting for game in various places, but nothing came into his hands at all, so when he reached Thum Klong Pain to rest he felt weak and disheartened. In the past he had hunted game in that district, so he had stayed in the cave before, but he never thought in the strange and peculiar way which he did this time.

Arriving at the cave added to his discouragement at not having seen any game, let alone having got any in his hands. He then started behaving very strangely in front of his companions, who were all hunters. He took the *Buddha Rūpas* which were spread about the cave and lined them up in several long rows. While doing this, he spoke in a loud voice, saying: "Today I looked for animals to shoot as game, but in the whole forest not one came into my hands. It must be because of these *Buddha Rūpas*. They must have put a spell on them and driven them far away from danger; that is, far from the hunters who were looking to shoot them. We must make these *Buddha Rūpas* line up military style and train them like soldiers so that they will learn the rules and regulations of hunters. Then these *Buddha Rūpas* will learn a lesson and won't make a spell to drive out all the animals anymore."

In his hand he held a stick which he used to beat the backs of the *Buddha Rūpas* that refused to accept his commands, lecturing all the *Buddha Rūpas* which he had set up in rows as though he was commanding rows of soldiers on parade. He ordered them to: "turn right, turn left, back step, march forward", while beating them on the back from time to time.

Occasionally, he beat one of them on the head, accusing it of not carrying out the orders of the commanding officer. If one of the *Buddha Rūpas* he was hitting fell over and went out of line, he picked it up and placed it back in line, while commanding: "turn right, turn left". He continued beating the *Buddha Rūpas* and scattering them about, then setting them in line again and giving them orders before beating them again, until the strength of his madness was finally exhausted. Then he stopped.

The other hunters there with him told him to stop right from the beginning, as soon as they saw his bad behaviour. They tried to reason with him, saying that he should not do such evil things. They warned him that he would fall into hell if he went on acting like that. They explained that each one of those *Buddha Rūpas* was there in place of the Buddha. To damage a *Buddha Rūpa* is considered by people to be the same as doing damage to the Lord Buddha — which is a very great evil that should never be done. The Lord Buddha and the *Buddha Rūpas* have a special place both in the hearts of people and in the hearts of *Devaputta, Devatā, Indra, Brahma, Yama, Yakkhas, Nāgas, Garuḍas, Pretas* and all kinds of ghosts as well, so they should never be desecrated.

But Master Baap Nah would not listen to any of it. He just went ahead and acted out his part. When the other hunters saw that it was no use reasoning with him, they one by one left the cave and ran back to their homes to tell people about that evil madness and the living denizen of hell who perpetrated it. The villagers all felt greatly dismayed, for they had never heard of such a thing happening before.

Before that hunter took the *Buddha Rūpas* and set them in rows to train them like soldiers, he had a normal awareness of things in the way most people have. In talking with others, he understood matters quite normally, so no one would have thought of him as being crazy. But he did possess the characteristic signs of hatred and aversion (*dosa*), which he displayed quite openly that day when he could not find and shoot any game. Thus he spoke angrily to the *Buddha Rūpas* saying that they were casting spells to drive all the game away. This is why he became angry with them and hit them and beat them in accordance with his emotional situation (*ārammaṇa*) without seeing at that time how his emotional situation was complete madness.

Throughout Thailand, everybody knows full well that *Buddha Rūpas* are not soldiers, nor are they cattle that one can grab them and train them or make them pull a plough or an ox cart. So why did that man dare to take those *Buddha Rūpas* and act towards them in such a repugnant way? He must have been crazier than people normally get in this world. It's something to consider. But if you prefer not to think about it, that will lighten the load on your mind so you won't go mad yourself thinking about that man who opened up the way to madness, thus inducing normal people to go a bit mad as well.

When his hellish madness had run its course, it broke up and disappeared. By the time he returned to his home he had become a good and normal person, but his tendency to lose his temper was still there. Nobody was bold enough to speak to him and question him, because they all knew about the incomparably evil things which he had done. So everyone kept quiet and acted as if nothing had happened, including those who lived with him in his house. But they kept a watch on him to see if there were any changes in him. The man himself wore a solemn expression but said nothing which would make them concerned or suspicious. So nobody was prepared to offend him by making an issue of what happened in the cave.

That night, as soon as it got dark, the hunter's family heard him complaining that his body was itching all over. They asked him what the problem was, and he showed them various places on his body that he said were so painfully hot that he could hardly stand it. He felt like shouting for help. When he showed them his body, both the parts under his clothes and those which were exposed, it was inflamed and swollen everywhere. It had all arisen quite suddenly in an unusual manner.

What with the pain, the swelling and the stinging heat coming so suddenly all together, he could hardly bear it and he cried out to people to come and help him, bursting into tears like a child. Word of what had happened spread quickly throughout the village, where everybody had heard about the despicable way he had behaved with the *Buddha Rūpas*. Many of them ran quickly to see for themselves, but still nobody was bold enough to speak the truth openly about what he had done to the *Buddha Rūpas* for fear that it may start something which would grow into serious trouble.

But an old man who was clever, esteemed and well-respected by all the villagers spoke out clearly so that the hunter would hear what he said:

"This kind of thing is something that we have never seen happen before, but is probably caused by some terribly evil occurrence, rather than anything else. You should reflect back on the recent past to see whether you have done anything which was not good and proper. Think back and examine what you have done. There may well be something there, for what has happened to you is most unusual. It doesn't normally happen to people. We have all seen rashes, and aches and pains, and hot stinging sensations in the body, but we have never seen them in such an unusual manner as you have them at present. Look at your body! This condition has spread out all over it like a fire, and so quickly too. Your body has suddenly broken out in rashes and swellings of a most abnormal kind. There must surely be something which has caused it to happen, for under ordinary circumstances this wouldn't happen. Using the colloquial way of speaking in the village, we would say it was caused by *kamma. Kamma* is what has brought this about and nothing else, so you should investigate and review what your actions have been, where you have been and what you have done."

It's normal for people to be careless and make mistakes. So the villagers began asking him questions while helping to look after his sickness, all the while watching the good and bad reactions of the sick person. At the same time, they asked around among the people present; first one person, then another, and so on, one by one. But most of the hunters who were there in the cave and actually saw what he did had no desire to visit his home at all. What he did had deeply disturbed them, so they felt that his evil actions were worse than could be settled by asking questions and making accusations to his face at a meeting of village elders. Even those hunters who did go to his home went quietly and looked on without letting the culprit see them at all, for they were afraid that it might cause some future trouble.

When he had been told about good and evil in various ways and had been questioned many times by people in a roundabout way, constantly bringing up the topics of merit and demerit, heaven and hell, he began to recall his own evil deeds and he realised the gravity of what he had done. He then told them all about all what he did with the *Buddha Rūpas* in Thum Klong Pain cave. As he spoke he was consciously aware of the moral significance of his actions, in the same way any normal person would be. There was no sign of insanity or anything abnormal concealed in him at all as he spoke. So as soon as the old man, whom everyone in the village as well as the hunter respected, saw a convenient opening, he pretended to be alarmed at what he heard and terrified of the consequences of such evil and the prospect of falling into hell, telling the hunter:

"All *Buddha Rūpas* stand in place of the Great Teacher, the foremost leader of this world, and they are focal points for the hearts of all Buddhists throughout the earth wherever Buddhism is established, as well as for countless numbers of *Devaputtas, Devatās, Indras, Brahmas, Yamas, Yakkhas, Nāgas, Garuḍas, Pretas* and ghosts. All of them pay homage to images of the Buddha. They cherish them greatly and protect them, preventing anyone from manhandling or damaging these sacred objects in any way. Each of those *Buddha Rūpas* in the cave had *Devatās, Nāgas* and *Garuḍas* guarding and looking after them all the time. Nobody can go and mess about with them without coming up against the *Devatās* who look after them, who will punish such a person in many possible ways, depending on the skill and ability in magic powers of those *Devatās*. The punishment will manifest in a manner that is appropriate to that person and to the strength of the *kamma* which that person has made by his aggressive actions.

"If the hunter has told the truth, then none of us need have doubt about what has happened. The 'fire' that is burning his body all over right now must be due to the bad thoughts and actions he directed toward those *Buddha Rūpas* for sure. Oh well, never mind. Now that we know the full reason for this quite clearly, we should be able to correct the situation and relieve this disorder so that he can return to normal. There is no reason why father (the old man) should not bring his son[3] to ask forgiveness for his faults from the Lord Buddha, the Dhamma and the Sangha, so that they may refrain from punishing him and allow him to quickly recover from this gruesome illness."

The hunter believed everything that the wise old man explained to him. He did not object at all and he smiled brightly. Everyone present could see that he looked fresh and happy.

The only problem that remained then was the reluctance of the hunter to ask forgiveness of the *Buddha Rūpas* in Thum Klong Pain cave while he remained in such discomfort, with heat rashes and intense itching. If he wasn't able to go to the cave, what should he do? Immediately the old man spoke in a soothing voice, saying:

"Never mind about that. Even though you cannot go there just yet, you can still ask the Buddha to forgive your faults without any problem. You can take any *Buddha Rūpa*, which stands in place of the Buddha, and place it in front of you, along with flowers and joss sticks. Then you must respectfully prostrate to the *Buddha Rūpa* and ask forgiveness for your faults. Do this first. Then, when you have overcome those painful symptoms, you must go and pay your respects to the *Buddha Rūpas* at Thum Klong Pain. Doing it in this way will bring the same result, have no fear."

After the old man had finished speaking, he told the people to bring a *Buddha Rūpa* and set it up in front of the sick hunter. Then they prompted him to ask forgiveness for his evil acts from that *Buddha Rūpa*. When he finished, he and everyone else felt quite relieved. The ceremony was done properly in all respects in the midst of hundreds of people from all over the village who had rushed in excitedly to witness this unprecedented event.

It was remarkable how the fact that evil exists, virtue exists, hell exists and heaven exists was so clearly displayed to all those people who knew what the hunter had done. They could see the results of his evil deeds with their own eyes and know them with their own hearts. His strange disorder began to gradually die away as soon as he accepted his faults and asked forgiveness from the *Buddha Rūpa*. After that, it cleared up very quickly; in fact, so quickly that it was most unusual. The hunter seemed to gain a new lease on life after he had battled the great champions, the *Buddha Rūpas* in Thum Klong Pain. He had learned his lesson well. He made a solemn vow in front of the *Buddha Rūpa* that he would never again do anything against the Buddha to the end of his life. He had seen clearly for himself the consequences of his actions, in a way that he would never forget.

In a few days the hunter's symptoms completely disappeared and he returned to normal. So he prepared flowers and joss sticks and went to ask forgiveness of the *Buddha Rūpas* in Thum Klong Pain, which he had previously looked upon as his trained soldiers. He prostrated to each one and asked forgiveness for his faults. He also made a solemn resolve that he would no longer be such a gross, despicable character as he was before. He even resolved to give up completely his occupation as a master hunter. He resolved never to hunt again for the rest of his life, with the understanding in his heart that: evil exists, merit exists, hell exists and heaven exists; that if one does good, one receives good, if one does evil, one receives evil. This hunter no longer had any doubts about this.

THE KILESAS ARE SAD, GLOOMY, CHEERLESS mental defilements which the wisest people, with the Lord Buddha as the best example, have always censured and decried as bad. They are truly a bane on the hearts of beings in the world, exactly as the Lord censured them. The *kilesas* are what rejects the true nature of Dhamma, making out that it is not true and that it has never existed. They never agree to accept the truth enough to be admired in any way. The *kilesas* share nothing in common with Dhamma, so they can never establish a state of Dhamma in the beings of this world over whom they have control. They deny the existence of good and evil and heaven and hell, just as they deny the existence of *Nibbāna*. So we should never think that the *kilesas* have a good aspect that confirms the existence of the Dhamma that the Lord Buddha taught. Rather, they negate its existence and try to blot it out altogether. Living beings that live in subjugation to the *kilesas* have no chance to believe in good and evil, and thus no incentive to renounce evil and develop virtue so as to work towards a heavenly existence in the future. Instead, they remain submerged in darkness and suffer continuously because the deceptive nature of the *kilesas* completely covers up the truth.

The *kilesas*, regardless of what type, are all descendents of the great master of deception who always deludes living beings, making them dull and stupid so that they remain firmly

147

under his control. This great deceiver makes them close off their senses and lie down passively while being totally subject to his power. The hunter Boon Nah was an excellent example in this present age. The *kilesas* snuck into his heart and started a fire there. Then they deceived the hunter into plunging into this fire wildly without any restraint, inducing him to take the *Buddha Rūpas*, which are exalted and sacred things in Dhamma, and train them as if they were soldiers while beating them in various ways. This continued until he met up with the good side — in other words, his body became inflamed and covered in swellings which were irritating and hot and visible for all to see. Not knowing whether he would live or die, he was getting ready to fall into hell at that time. Just at that moment, the son of a *Deva* (the old man) came to help him, leading him to see the evil in what he had done. This intervention allowed him to turn back to the way of Dhamma so that he accepted the truth about the existence of good and evil. Thus he escaped that time from the danger of disaster, as he avoided having those sinister *kilesas* drag him down into hell even while he was still alive.

All of us Buddhists should therefore examine and reflect on the truth of the principles of Dhamma which that wise old man taught. As well, we should reflect well on the falseness of the *kilesas* which are always whispering their deceitful words within our hearts. We shouldn't think only of profit, we shouldn't think only of cheating others, we shouldn't always think of ourselves first — for that attitude results in others losing their wealth and property, which damages their hearts and kindles the fires of hell in our own hearts.

The Dhamma of the wise teaches that we should be afraid of those things that Dhamma teaches us to fear, such as evil; and that we should be bold in those things where we should have confidence, such as virtue and merit. This teaching is correct, for it conforms entirely to the truth without any falsehood or error. It contains no deviation from truth such is found in the deceptive tricks of all the *kilesas*. Whoever believes in the *kilesas* will be entirely ruined without any likelihood of recovery or improvement, which only firm faith in the Dhamma can provide.

The wise always feel repugnance and loathing for the *kilesas*; none of them have any love or attachment for the *kilesas*. In contrast to this, those who have faith in the *kilesas* and their deceptive tricks, which teach them to disdain and negate Dhamma, are eventually consumed by fire. As for the *kilesas* which deceive those people, they don't accept any part of the evil *kamma*; instead, the *kilesas* just keep on deceiving people, causing them to sink deeper and deeper all the time.

So I ask you to please examine yourselves well, in a manner which is appropriate to your state as intelligent human beings who are 'children' of the Lord Buddha, who was supremely wise, clever and skilled beyond all the *kilesas* of every kind and was never deluded by any of their tricks. We Buddhists should try to follow in the footsteps of the Great Teacher by being careful and cautious on all sides in every situation, including everything that comes into contact with us through the eyes, ears, nose, tongue, body and mind. Don't give way and let the *kilesas* grab you and throw you down a chasm, for it will ruin this auspicious human birth of yours. By not admiring what is good, you allow yourself to go to ruin in this life, which is most inappropriate for all of us who have the teaching of Dhamma ringing loud in our ears to help us all the time. For we have teachers, many environments suitable for meditation, and an abundance of books and scriptures to help us overcome the *kilesas*. So we cannot say that Dhamma is lacking or in short supply.

Dhamma can always keep up with the *kilesas*; it is never at a loss in this regard. It can revolve around every aspect of oneself, successfully resisting the *kilesas* at every turn and in every corner, so you shouldn't be reluctant to use Dhamma to help yourself go in the right direction. Instead, you should be afraid of the *kilesas*, which lead only in the direction of evil and suffering, and never in the direction of happiness. They lead a person to lose all hope even though he is still alive and breathing. This should certainly never happen to us. So don't be complacent! Don't look on dangers as if they were virtues! Don't look on merit and virtue as being bad and evil! From now on you must take a lesson from your past actions and the resultant *dukkha*, and never make those same mistakes again. You will then be a good person who progresses in happiness — *sugato* — without a doubt, in accordance with the Dhamma verse that the Lord taught: "Dhamma looks after those who practise Dhamma, not letting them fall into evil ways".

This story of Master Hunter Boon Nah became very widely known, both in that district and in other places far distant from it. Many who heard it were afraid. They no longer dared to trample carelessly around that cave as they had before. The cave and its surroundings then became a quiet and lonely place well suited to the practice of meditation and the ascetic mode of living of all *Dhutanga Kammaṭṭhāna Bhikkhus*. The villagers in that district considered it to be a sacred place, so they did not dare to do as they pleased there like they used to.

Pure Moral Virtues

It was then that Ajaan Khao, who was taking his disciples out wandering in the way of *Dhutanga Kammaṭṭhāna*, decided to stop and stay at Thum Klong Pain cave to develop the practice of Dhamma. He saw that it was a convenient and peaceful place well-suited to the needs of the body, the mind and the practice of *Samaṇa-dhamma*. It also had a beneficial influence on the sharpness and subtlety of his meditation. So he decided to stay at Wat Thum Klong Pain continually until the end of his life.

He spent the rest of his life looking after the Bhikkhus and novices at Wat Thum Klong Pain, teaching all of them steadily without ever giving up. The Dhamma which he liked to teach them started off with constant training in the four moral purities — *catu-pārisuddhi-sīla*:

Indriya-saṁvara-sīla

This means the restraint of and watchfulness over the six *indriya*: the eyes, ears, nose, tongue, body and mind. Not letting them give rise to pleasure or displeasure which arouses love and hate, loathing, anger, greed and craving for those things which contact the senses, without ever reaching satisfaction and sufficiency. The six internal sense fields — *āyatana* — which are the eye, ear, nose, tongue, body and mind, together with the six external sense fields, which are: form, sound, smell, taste, things which make contact with the body, and mental objects that come from things which make contact with the mind — form pairs in which the internal and external sense fields act together (as the eye does with form, for example). This contact easily creates problems that are very difficult to get rid of.

So Ajaan Khao taught that those who are ordained to practise Dhamma to free themselves from all *dukkha* should always be very careful whenever any pair of these *āyatana*, or all of them together, go inward and make contact with the heart. They should not allow the internal *āyatana* — such as the eyes — to make contact with the corresponding external *āyatana* — such as form — without having mindfulness constantly in their hearts.

Those who set up their minds to be restrained and watchful in accordance with the teaching of the Lord Buddha are those who train themselves for the steady process of washing out the *kilesas*. They are not slow and hesitant in walking the path, so they will reach the shore of safety before long. But for all those who practise the way without going through to the end, they will generally tend to remain submerged groping about in *dukkha*. They simply let a giant demon[4] gobble them up along the way (while they are still practising the way of Dhamma) because they don't have any restraint or any interest in being careful. Although they have little mindfulness and wisdom, they want to see results before doing the work. So they venture out into the demon's territory (the field of the countless emotional problems which are a danger to them). First they lose restraint, then carefulness and mindfulness disappear in the 'jungle', leaving such people to fight the 'tiger' with their bare hands. Finally, they climb up onto the 'chopping block' and let the *kilesas* of *ragataṇhā* (sexual craving) chop them up and make a delicious meal out of them. The only thing that stands out prominently is their own incompetence.

For this reason, restraint in the six sense faculties (*indriya*) is an essential task for those who are ordained and practise the way. Those who have already done some of this practice will know about it for themselves without there being any need to tell them. No other task is as arduous as this one. But if it is hard, so be it; if it is difficult, so be it. Setting up an attitude of restraint and carefulness in one's heart is bound to be a major task in all situations. It means fighting in order to extract the *kilesas*, which are like arrows stuck in the heart. It means battling the strength of the *kilesas* which are pouring into the six internal sense fields, as well as cleaning out and uprooting those *kilesas* that dwell in the heart which are continually creating trouble and restlessness there.

No other task is more arduous than destroying and cleaning out the *kilesas*. There is nothing more difficult than the task of extracting those *kilesas* that fuel the fire which burns and smoulders in the heart all the time. The Lord Buddha, the foremost of all wise men, placed this task at the highest level of importance and value. Whoever learns this task to completion is supreme in a way that requires no confirmation from anyone else, for the supremacy of his virtue exists on its own as a natural principle of Dhamma, which he knows for himself by way of *Sandiṭṭhiko*[5] — having no doubt what it is.

The task of restraining these sense faculties could, at the time of the Lord Buddha, arouse a sense of competition. This is because anyone who guards even one of the fields of sensation finds it difficult. It is as if they don't have any other fields of sense, so it seems to them as if guarding any of the other fields of sense could not be as difficult as the one they are guarding. For example, the *Pañcabhikkhu* — the five Bhikkhus who each guarded one of his fields of sense. The first guarded only his eyes whenever they came into association with any visible form. The next guarded only his ears whenever they heard any sound. The next guarded only his nose whenever he smelt anything. The next guarded only his tongue whenever he tasted anything. The last one guarded only his body whenever anything cold or hot, soft or hard made contact with it. None of them guarded all the fields of sense. When they got together to discuss their experiences, each of them boasted that the field of sense that he was guarding was more difficult to guard than any of the others. This led to arguments and disagreements, because none of them were ready to concede that the others could find it as difficult to do as they themselves did, and none of them would accept that all the fields of sense were equally difficult to guard. In the end, the Lord Buddha came and expounded the Dhamma to them, teaching them that each of the fields of sense was equally difficult to guard, saying:

"The eye likes to see beautiful and attractive forms. The ear likes to hear sounds that are beautiful, melodious and pleasing to the heart. The nose likes to smell things that are pleasantly scented, making one feel joyful. The tongue likes to taste things that are delicious. The body likes to touch and feel things that are soft and smooth, which produces a state of absorbed fascination all the time without ever having too much of it.

"All of this originates from the heart, which is the 'over-lord' of all these fields of sense. The heart is the one that wants to play about with them all the time without being the least bit concerned to consider what is right or wrong, what is good or bad. All the heart wants is what fulfils its desires. This makes all the fields of sense, including the eye, ear, nose, tongue and body, whirl about according to the emotional dictates of the heart (that is, the emotional dictates of the *kilesas* force the heart to struggle).

"When guarding each sense field, we must keep a guard on the heart at the same time. The heart is the ringleader which constantly creates the desire to see sights, to hear sounds, to smell scents, to taste foods and to feel contacts. The heart is the one that desires, that craves, that is hungry and thirsty, the one that goes searching for sensations. So the heart uses its instruments, which are the eyes, ear, nose, tongue and body, as the paths by which it travels out to search for all sorts of *ārammana*.

"So you must guard the heart with mindfulness and inves-tigate it carefully with wisdom. Don't let it roam about getting involved in things which are dangerous. Use mindfulness to control the heart; use wisdom to investigate and examine the *ārammana* that arise from making contact with forms, sounds, smells, tastes and things which contact the body, so as to learn the truth of such things. Then the heart will remain detached and indifferent. It will not love some things and hate others, and so become angry. It will then easily enter into a state of calm and peacefulness without being burdened or troubled by external matters. When the *citta* is replete and satisfied in that calm state, it will withdraw from it and examine the internal sense fields of the eyes, ears, nose, tongue and body as being merely instruments of the heart. It will then examine those *ārammaṇa* in relation to the heart, seeing that they both become intimately blended together, as though they were one and the same thing.

"The examination of the physical body may be done in whatever way you find most suitable: either by examining its repulsiveness (*asubha*), or by seeing its impermanence (*anicca*), its unsatisfactoriness (*dukkha*), or its lack of any self-principle (*anattā*), or by dividing it up into the elements (*dhātu*) or groups (*khandhas*), whichever one finds most suitable and easiest to do. The examination of the body is important because initially the *ārammaṇa* of the heart tend to be bound up with external things such as visible forms. So you must analyse this relationship, going back and forward to see how it works until you understand all about *ārammaṇa*. You will see that they are things which infiltrate the heart, and so are not one and the same thing as the heart. Go on investigating until you gain an understanding of how the external and internal sense fields work, using mindfulness, wisdom, faith and effort relentlessly without weakening. When you have completely examined all aspects of it, whatever is false will drop away from the heart and whatever is true will be a trusted companion of the heart that supports it and enables it to do its work with ease and skill right through to the end of the road so that nothing will be able to obstruct it anymore."

When the Lord Buddha finished giving this teaching about guarding the sense fields, all five of those Bhikkhus attained the level of *Arahantship* directly from the Great Teacher. They finished the task and no longer needed to act like convicts in prison watchfully guarding their sense faculties all the time. All quarrels and arguments between them also stopped at the same time.

Thus it is that the sense faculties in association with the six sense fields are things which are always very difficult to guard. In fact, nothing can compare with it, because these are the avenues by which all the most powerful *kilesas* push their influence and get their own way. If you don't have mindfulness to thoroughly look after yourself, and wisdom to skilfully sort out what is happening when the *kilesas* pour out through one of these pathways, you are bound to fall flat on your back every time. Nobody can rightly boast that they have gained the exceptional ability needed to attain 'Buddha purity' by letting go of all bodily restraint and letting the mind go where it will. For that reason, the four moral purities (*pārisuddhi-sīla*) are essential *dhammas* that are very important amongst Buddhists, especially amongst those who practise the way.

I myself don't dare to act so boldly with the *kilesas*, for I lack these *dhammas* as weapons to fight with them. Without these *dhammas*, no amount of bravery can defeat them. Those who have freed themselves from the *kilesas* are the most persistent and resolute of warriors who have reached the goal of the religious life (*Brahmacariyā*) by using these *dhammas*. In doing so, they have become the most exalted of individuals whom the world bows down and pays homage to as the highest examples of spiritual attainment.

Paṭimokkha-saṁvara-sīla

This moral purity involves being self-controlled and guarded with respect to the moral behaviour expressed in the *Paṭimokkha*[6]. It means not transgressing or resisting any of the rules, whether minor or major. This ensures that the manners and the behaviour of those who are ordained shall be good and seemly.

There are 227 rules in the *Paṭimokkha*, but there are also a large number of minor rules that the Buddha established from time to time that appear outside the *Paṭimokkha*. In fact, those rules in the *Paṭimokkha* are a small proportion of the total number of rules, which altogether number in the thousands. Those who are good pupils, following in the footsteps of the teacher — which means the Great Teacher — will have a reverent attitude to the moral precepts which are to be found in the *Vinaya*, for the *Vinaya* stands in the place of the Great Teacher.

Avijjā-pārisuddhi-sīla

This moral purity entails the livelihood of a Bhikkhu who is a follower of the *Tathāgata* (the Buddha). For example, a Bhikkhu walks on the alms round, going on foot to the village each day to receive his food. He does not use tricks, fraud or deception to get his food. A Bhikkhu also obtains all of his four basic requisites in a pure way, meaning that the one who gives does so with a pure heart knowing that the one who receives has come looking for it in a pure manner, not with some ulterior motive as is done in the world at large. He searches for it in the manner of a Bhikkhu, partakes of it in the manner of a

Bhikkhu, lives in the manner of a Bhikkhu, and uses the four requisites in the manner of a Bhikkhu, fully and completely, without extravagance, pride, vanity, intemperance or arrogance. He dwells in the Dhamma of contentment, which is the basic level of living and progressing of a Bhikkhu who has the *sīla* of pure livelihood as the ornament that decorates his status.[7] Whether he is in want or he has plenty, he is seemly in his status and never goes beyond the bounds of what is proper for a Bhikkhu. It is this Dhamma of right livelihood which adorns the mouth, the stomach and the status of a Bhikkhu, making his behaviour always pleasing and attractive.

Paccaya-sannissita-sīla

This moral purity means that a Bhikkhu must be self-controlled and restrained in respect to the four requisites[8] which he depends on. He must not be capricious or whimsical in his choice of food or any of the other requisites, which opens the way for other baneful blemishes to flow in.

The requisites that a recluse depends on are of four kinds:

1. The robes which he wears in his status as a Bhikkhu. They should be the right size for him and dyed with a yellowish-brown colour which the Lord called *kāsāva* (the 'yellow' robe). A Bhikkhu must always have three robes without fail. They are the *Cīvara* (the main robe), the *Saṅghāṭi* (the outer robe) and the *Antaravāsaka* (the lower robe). Apart from these there are various other auxiliary pieces of cloth such as the '*angsa*' (a kind of under shirt), the bathing cloth and various other pieces used for certain necessities.

2. *Piṇḍapāta* is the category concerned with food. This means basic foods that people everywhere rely upon for sustenance to keep them going from day to day. It includes all those foods that a Bhikkhu is allowed to eat according to the *Vinaya* rules.

3. Bhikkhus must depend upon a dwelling place (*senāsana*) much as people in the world do. It is the place where they live, lie down to rest and sleep, and practise the way of *Samaṇa-dhamma* in all activities. That place should suit the temperament of someone who is not restless and agitated, such as living at the foot of a tree, at the mouth of a cave, under an overhanging cliff, in a forest, on a mountain side, on a mountain ridge, at the foot of a mountain, in a charnel ground or in a small hut in the thick jungle — any place which is sufficient to give some cover to rest, sleep and practise Dhamma by day and night. These are what are meant by a 'dwelling place'. In other words, it is a suitable place to live for a Bhikkhu whose purpose in ordaining is to practise meditation for the sake of Dhamma, for the Path, Fruition and *Nibbāna*, and for gaining true freedom. For a Bhikkhu who has these purposes in mind, the above dwelling places will provide a suitable place to live and practise well.

If we were to hold a competition among various kinds of dwelling places, making the Lord Buddha the judge instead of the *kilesas*, dwellings would surely be rated according to the principles of Dhamma, not according to how expensive, opulent, well-built and lasting they are. Beautiful and expensive dwellings with many floors, many rooms and many passageways would not get high marks. For the dwelling places which were favourably rated in the time of the Lord Buddha were those listed above. Beginning with the Lord Buddha and continuing through all the *Sāvakas*, there has never been any disagreement on this issue, which has been displayed in the Dhamma teachings for all to see. All subsequent generations have read these teachings, studied them and put them into practice, following on from teacher to pupil, right up to the present day.

In most cases, the refuges (*saraṇa*) that Buddhists gain within themselves arise from those dwelling places that are replete with qualities which promote only Dhamma, like the ones described above. Such places are suitable for the life and daily practice of someone who truly sees the danger in the round of *saṁsāra* within his heart. Buddha, Dhamma and Sangha are likely to arise in those places, for they can arise more easily there than in places that cause restlessness and agitation. Disturbing, restless places are almost certain to be fertile ground for the cultivation and promotion of the *kilesas*, for the development of the 'round of *kamma*' and the 'round of *vipāka*' (the results of *kamma*), which like a wheel spins round and round in a circle with no apparent way out — like a red ant circling around the outer edge of a winnowing basket.[9]

To summarise, the dwelling places which the Lord Buddha recommended, of which dwelling at the foot of a tree is an example, are places that are fully appropriate to the present day. They support and encourage one's efforts to drive out the *kilesas* by pushing them into a corner, destroying them and quickly dispersing them from the heart. Therefore, when a man is being newly ordained as a Bhikkhu, his preceptor is required to teach him which dwelling places are suitable for the life of a monk. This has always been the case with every Bhikkhu who is ordained, from the time of the Buddha to the present day. Never in that time has dwelling at the foot of a tree been considered out-of-date. Except, perhaps, in cases where Bhikkhus are overwhelmed by the *kilesas*, which drag them along and force them to consider it old-fashioned.

So there has never been any objection to the 'well-taught Dhamma' (*Svākkhāta dhamma*) by those who aim to know and see Dhamma in the heart by means of the practice of *citta bhāvanā*, following the path of the Great Teacher and what he taught. For the practice that he taught tends to blend in well with their preference for dwelling at the foot of a tree, in a cave, under an overhanging cliff, in a charnel ground or in thick forest. These places are suitable because they encourage the putting forward of effort more so than any other type of place. This includes those costly places which worldly people consider good, such as city centres and shopping malls. This is because Dhamma and those who search for Dhamma are different from most people in the world, even though they may come from the same social background, because their thinking and their understanding are quite different. Therefore, the places that are favoured by followers of Dhamma — such as those mentioned above — are places that are always suitable for the steady and continuous practice of Dhamma. They are not old-fashioned or out-of-date; rather, they are battlefields of victory where people can constantly do battle with the various kinds of *kilesas* until the sky and the earth disintegrate (until faith in the *Sāsana dhamma* disappears completely from people's hearts).

4. *Gilāna-bhesajja* means medicines which people throughout the world normally use for curing sickness. The nature of a

Bhikkhu's body is similar to that of people everywhere — they both have the same requirements so far as food and medicines are concerned. At the time of the Lord Buddha, however, they had few medicines, unlike nowadays when we have many. Even the diseases probably weren't as strange and unusual as the ones people have nowadays, since they arose mostly due to natural causes found in their immediate environment. So in the early teachings of Buddhism, the only medicines recommended for Bhikkhus were pickled urine and a few herbal remedies. There were not many medicines then, like nowadays when they have become goods which flood the market. Today the population is very high, so there are many diseases, many doctors, many medicines, and many people who die of diseases that the medicines and the doctors cannot cure. In past ages, there was a low population, people had little and there was less disease, so there were few medicines, and deaths due to unusual and strange diseases were rare. Because of that, people were not concerned about medicines and doctors like they are nowadays.

According to the ancient Buddhist scriptures, Bhikkhus at the time of the Lord Buddha showed little concern or anxiety for dangerous diseases and painful fevers. There is no indication that they took medicines along with them when they travelled. The most that they took along, if they took anything at all, was yellow myrobalan and emblic myrobalan[10] to cure the feelings of physical weakness and tiredness that occasionally arose. But they always considered the Path, Fruition and *Nibbāna* to be the surest remedy of all. Their minds were more likely to go in the direction of Dhamma in order to transcend the world, rather than succumbing to the fear of dangerous diseases, painful fevers and death, and then searching for medicines to cure them. They had little fear of death, but they had great fear of failing to get free of the *kilesas* and the great mass of *dukkha*. Day and night, in all their activities, the Bhikkhus of that day were fully engaged in the practice of Dhamma. Their faith, their effort, their mindfulness, their *samādhi* and their wisdom were all fully engaged in the practice of Dhamma. Then if a danger-ous and painful fever arose in them, those Bhikkhus would be most likely to examine it in the light of Dhamma truth which, in effect, turns into a medicine that both cures the fever and destroys the *kilesas* at the same time. They did not weakly de-pend on medicines and doctors as their main life support. They used them only as was reasonably appropriate for a Bhikkhu who has faith in Dhamma, faith in *kamma* and faith in the Dhamma truths as being always true and unchanging. Under normal conditions, those Bhikkhus were calm and pleasing to look at. When they had a painful illness they did not suddenly lose their composure and start writhing about in pain uncon-trollably, discarding that exemplary behaviour that is seemly and appropriate for a recluse. Instead, they had mindfulness as their companion, so they were not heavy-hearted or depressed. They never forgot the Dhamma they had in their hearts.

Even today, *Dhutanga Kammaṭṭhāna Bhikkhus* practice in the same way as those Bhikkhus at the time of the Lord Buddha when they are afflicted with painful ailments. They are less concerned about their sickness and whether it will be cured or not, or whether they will live or die, than they are about their investigation into the Dhamma truths. They are more interested in understanding the true nature of the body, the painful feeling, memory (*saññā*) and imaginative thought (*sankhāra*), which deceive the *citta* at that time. By this understanding, they destroy the *kilesas* at the same time. In doing so, they entrust their health and well-being to those Dhamma truths that appear in connection with the illness and the pain at that time. At the same time, they consider the deceptive tricks of their minds which have been instigated by *kilesas* to be very important. In the investigation, mindfulness and wisdom must take note of those deceptive tricks, and also maintain contact with the pain, with the body and with the heart, all of which are interrelated. The purpose of the investigation is to use wisdom to know and understand clearly the true nature of all these factors in order to gradually let go of attachment to them as mindfulness and wisdom discover the truth.

Bhikkhus do use medicines to cure sickness, but they prefer to use the 'Dhamma remedy', which is the one that attacks and destroys the *kilesas* at the same time. They do not merely lie down keeping a watch over their pain as they wait for medicines to cure them, or weakly call out for people to help them recover. Instead, they call on faith, effort, mindfulness, *samādhi* and wisdom to help cure their sickness, and help destroy the *kilesas* at the same time. The result is the realisation that sickness is merely something which arises in the body, and not something which should be allowed to pierce and enter their hearts. So their hearts remain strong in their faith in the Dhamma truths, which they see clearly in themselves. Mindfulness and wisdom are then fully proficient within them and they are not afraid of suffering or death, so they are contented and free from anxiety and concern. This is what is meant when we say that present-day *Dhutanga Kammaṭṭhāna Bhikkhus* treat illness with the 'Dhamma remedy', which is the way it's usually done in the sphere of the Dhamma truths.

Benefiting the World

Venerable Ajaan Khao had many followers including Bhikkhus, novices and lay people from many areas of Thailand. They came continually to learn and train in moral behaviour with him. But when he grew old, he tried to look after himself by being quiet and calm more than he used to do when he was younger. In that way, his mind and body would last as long as reasonably possible, so that he could give value to the world in the many places which needed to receive it.

Normally, after having eaten food in the morning, Ajaan Khao went to his *caṅkama* path and walked in meditation for one or two hours. Then he returned to his hut to rest, after which he sat in meditation until two o'clock in the afternoon. If he had no other business to attend to, he again went to his *caṅkama* path and continued walking meditation until it was time for him to sweep the ground in the open areas of the monastery. Following sweeping, he had a bath, after which he again walked *caṅkama* until ten or eleven p.m. He stopped then and returned to his hut, where he did some chanting and meditation until it was time for him to lie down and rest his body. He normally rose at about three a.m. and continued doing meditation until dawn, when it was time to go out for *piṇḍapāta*. After *piṇḍapāta*, he ate food to support his body, a result (*vipāka*) of his past *kamma* which he still had to look after. That is the daily routine that Ajaan Khao always maintained, unless some other essential business forced a change; such as, being asked to participate in various functions, causing a break in his routine.

Even in old age he still refused to allow his declining health to curtail his customary zeal. Some people have asked me why he continued to put such strenuous effort into practice when in truth he had nothing further to accomplish. They could not figure out why he remained so active and energetic. I tried to explain to them that someone who has completely eliminated the *kilesas* has no debilitating lethargy left to entrap his mind in a web of delusion. Meanwhile, the rest of us have amassed such a debilitating mountain of laziness that it virtually obscures us from view. As soon as we get started on some worthwhile endeavour, we become apprehensive lest the fruits of our efforts overload our capacity to store them. We worry ahead of time about how exhausted we will be when the work becomes difficult. In the end, having failed to gather those wholesome fruits, we are left with an empty basket; that is, an empty joyless heart, drifting aimlessly with no hard-earned store of merit to fall back on. Instead, we fill our empty hearts with complaints about all the difficulties we face. So laziness, this blight in our hearts, keeps throwing up obstacles to block our way. Those who have cleansed this blight from their hearts remain persistent, persevering in times of hardship. They never worry about overloading their capacity to store the fruits of their efforts. Those individuals whose hearts are pure, unblemished Dhamma, cleared of all worldly defilements, stand out majestically in all situations. Sombre, sullen moods never arise in their hearts, making them perfect examples for the world to follow.

People with Dhamma virtue as high as that of Ajaan Khao never expect to get happiness from any source other than from the Dhamma within their own hearts. Their lives are fulfilled by the Dhamma within them. Whatever their circumstances of life happen to be, their hearts have an unvarying happiness that neither increases nor decreases, unlike worldly people whose happiness fluctuates, having ups and downs that go together as a pair. The reason for this difference is that those *ajaans* have only one state of heart, one that is entirely pure throughout, having only Dhamma as its one state (*ekibhāva*) without any duality present to vie for recognition. This is a state of peace and happiness that is quite impossible to compare with anything else. The *citta* which is entirely pure throughout has peace and happiness that is sufficient in and of itself. It has no desire for any additional support, which would only be a useless disturbance that would be of no value at all to that *citta*.

For that reason, those whose *cittas* are pure like to live alone without distractions or disturbances. Disruptive conditions interrupt the calm and happiness in their basic nature, which is totally satisfied within itself, by causing the mind to stir and acknowledge the sensations that enter through the sense doors. So the *ajaans* prefer to seclude themselves in those places that are best suited to their natural dispositions. Those people who don't understand their reason for doing this, tend to think that the *ajaans* don't welcome visitors, or that they dislike people, or that they are only interested in saving themselves and are not interested in teaching and training others. But the fact of the matter is what has been explained above.

It is very rare to find anyone like these *ajaans* who can teach and train people with a completely pure heart full of *mettā*, without any thought of worldly gain or recompense. They teach people of every social status and every age group after having truly realised the truth within themselves. Teaching

Dhamma with *mettā* that is completely blameless, they aim to benefit those who accept the truth from them. The exception is those people who go to them and cause trouble by acting in ways that go beyond what is reasonable. When this happens, the *ajaan* will probably not welcome them or teach them. It's simply impossible for a Bhikkhu to do what is unreasonable by acting in accordance with the request of someone who knows no bounds in what is good and correct. Such a disturbance might cause him harm as well, which would be a shame.

WHILE VENERABLE AJAAN KHAO WAS STILL ALIVE, he kindly gave encouragement to large numbers of Bhikkhus and novices, as well as to lay people from many districts of Thailand. They came in a steady stream to pay homage to him and listen to his teaching. The Bhikkhus in his Wat saw that it was becoming increasingly difficult for him because he was getting old and his body was weak, so they arranged it so that visitors could only pay homage and receive his teaching at suitable times each day. This enabled him to get enough rest so that he could give benefit to the world for a long time, ensuring that his life would not be cut short before reaching its proper time.

For the most part, the meeting and receiving of guests for a Bhikkhu who is an *ajaan* involves meeting many lay people from many different backgrounds who have many preconceived ideas. The *ajaan* is usually the one who gets 'battered and bruised' the whole time while these people are with him. Most visitors are anxious to unload what is in their hearts on him, without considering whether they are making difficulties for him, or whether he has other duties which he should be doing at that time. So he tends to be disturbed more often than well water. If he doesn't meet their expectations, they become sullen and think that he's conceited and has an aversion for people because he refuses to receive guests in the way that one who is ordained as a Bhikkhu for the purpose of cleansing the *kilesas* of 'conceit' and 'aversion' should. Besides this, they also set up an attitude of dislike within themselves, which they spread out to others in many places, bringing harm to themselves and others all the time. Then, a Bhikkhu who should be revered, respected and beneficial to other people may become one who has a charge against him without any court that is capable of clearing him.

In truth, Bhikkhus are ordained for the purpose of bringing benefit to themselves as well as to the world to the best of their ability without being complacent. They do one kind of work at this time and another kind of work at that time, so they rarely have any spare time day or night. They must find time for helping the world, and time for helping the Bhikkhus and novices whom they look after, and all the rest of those who associate with them. They must also find time for the needs of their bodies and their minds so that they can live a long time and continue to bring benefit to the world. Every day and night their bodies and minds whirl round like a flywheel, giving them no time for rest and relaxation. When we think about it, even machines like motor vehicles are given time for rest, or for repair and maintenance, to extend their useful life. Otherwise, they would soon break up and be scrapped.

Bhikkhus are not bags of bricks or cement which can be used as building materials for constructing a house or a shop, wherever the master builder sees fit to use them. If it's like that,

Bhikkhus are bound to become exhausted and need a rest so they can put down the burden that makes them feel tense the whole time, giving them time to physically and mentally relax.

When lay people visit a Bhikkhu, they tend to bring along their usual temperament and their emotional problems as they please. Then they load it on him and make a lot of trouble for him, hoping he will make allowances for them. They never consider whether what they are doing is right or wrong, because fundamentally they have never been inclined to consider their behaviour in terms of right and wrong or good and bad. When they want a Bhikkhu to help them out with a problem, they rarely consider that Bhikkhus have customs and standards of behaviour that are different from theirs. Bhikkhus have the principles of Dhamma and *Vinaya* as the basis of their behaviour and their way of living. So the manners they display are those of the Dhamma and *Vinaya*, which require them to think in terms of right and wrong, good and bad all the time. Thus they must always consider carefully whether what they are asked to do is something they should or should not agree to.

Lay people are not likely to have Dhamma and *Vinaya* ingrained in them as their guiding principles, so generally they tend to believe in what they like and then practise accordingly. When they go to a Bhikkhu with this attitude, they are likely to disturb and trouble him, and perhaps do him some harm, even though they have no intention to do so. Or maybe they harm him indirectly by, for example, asking him to tell them the winning number of the state lottery, which violates the Dhamma and *Vinaya* of a Bhikkhu; asking him to make up magic potions to make a man and a woman love each other; asking him to tell them the auspicious time when their luck is good for becoming wealthy, or for any one of a thousand other desires which they may have; asking him to predict their future by astrology; asking him to tell them a magic saying or mantra to protect them so that they can withstand anyone who comes to mug them, or so they can't be shot, stabbed or clubbed; or asking him to make 'holy water' to ward off misfortune, distress, evil and dangers. Such actions are contrary to the traditional values of the Dhamma and *Vinaya* that Bhikkhus uphold, so they should not go along with such requests.

In addition, the more revered an *ajaan* is, the more he is troubled by things like the foregoing requests, and many others of the same sort; in fact, so many that it would take all day to describe them. *Dhutanga Bhikkhus* in the lineage of Venerable Ajaan Mun whose aim is the attainment of liberation have no interest in the above things and consider them to be enemies to their progress on the path of the right Dhamma. They are the kinds of activities that lead people to develop very bad principles in themselves, ones that can even openly destroy Bhikkhus and the religion they practise. For example, they may call a Bhikkhu the 'lottery Bhikkhu' or the 'magic potion Bhikkhu'; and Buddhism they may call 'the lottery religion' or 'the magic potion religion'. This becomes a stain and a blemish on the Bhikkhus and on Buddhism that steadily reduces its value. It's an inevitable consequence of agreeing to requests such as those mentioned above.

I have no intention to blame those faithful people found everywhere who go to meet Bhikkhus out of a love of Dhamma. Rather, my intention is to inform people about the situation so they may know the right and proper way of doing things between Bhikkhus and lay people, who can never be completely separated. When each side knows how to behave properly in relation to the other, their relationship becomes harmonious and straight-forward. This conforms with the concern for virtue and for the welfare of the religion which both sides share as they entrust their lives and their well-being to each other.

The Burden of the Khandhas

Beginning the 18th January 1967, Venerable Ajaan Khao became very sick. It started out as a cold and a fever. But the characteristics of the fever changed and fluctuated in a variety of different ways which caused other diseases to get in and develop and gain strength until he was unable to eat any food. In the beginning, when it was only a cold with a fever, he continued to make the effort to eat food with the other Bhikkhus and novices at the front of the cave in Wat Thum Klong Pain. People who saw him there may have thought that he was simply suffering the effects of old age, as is common with old people. But because of the increasing complications brought on by the changes in his disease, the strength of his body deteriorated day after day until eventually he could not go and eat food with the others in the cave. He continued to put up with the difficulties, forcing himself to eat a little food in his hut each day, until finally he was unable to eat anything at all. Gradually his strength became visibly weaker until he had to rely upon the Bhikkhus who were looking after him to help him every time he wanted to move.

When news of Ajaan Khao's condition reached the surrounding area, waves of lay people and Bhikkhus from that district rushed to the Wat to see him. In their hearts many people firmly believed in him as a refuge they could confidently entrust their lives to. So when they heard that he was seriously ill, they were very perturbed — as if the sky and earth had collapsed and their hearts had been torn from their bodies. After the news had been broadcast, people came in hoards from all directions, lay people as well as Bhikkhus and novices. They came to visit Ajaan Khao to see how he was. They were very eager to meet him and to pay their respects to him.

For that reason, it appeared as if there was some large function taking place at Wat Thum Klong Pain while Ajaan Khao was sick. So many Bhikkhus and lay people came from so many different places that the Wat was unable to look after them all. There was not enough bedding or food and other necessities to go around. So they just had to help themselves and each other as best they could to make up for what was lacking. A Wat is a place to live for Bhikkhus, who rely on the local villagers for the food they receive on alms round. It is not a place where wealthy people live, which most people already know. One advantage of Wat Thum Klong Pain is that it is very large, with lots of forest and hills and plenty of shady trees. There are also a number of overhanging cliffs. It is all together quite a good place to stay if one takes the forest, the hills and the shady trees in the Wat as one's accommodation, where one can just rest and sleep, relaxed and unconcerned.

Even though there were large numbers of people to feed, there was always plenty of food given to the Bhikkhus on their daily alms round. From the start right through to the end of his illness, a period of over four months, amazingly there was never insufficient food. Probably this was largely influenced by the protective power of Ajaan Khao's great virtue. All the many lay people, Bhikkhus and novices who gathered together there seemed to be like children of the same parents or members of the same family. They stayed together quietly and peacefully, without anyone controlling them and without any untoward incidents occurring. They were all cheerful and smiling when meeting one another, talking together in a mild and pleasant manner, as if they had often met together and known each other for a long time.

When Ajaan Khao first became ill, several senior *ajaans* met to discuss the possibility of a disturbance to the peaceful atmosphere in the Wat with so many monks and lay people staying together. They were also eager to maintain discipline among the Bhikkhus and novices who came into the Wat so as to promote peace and harmony in their association with each other and to foster an attitude of carefulness among all of them. The whole occasion passed off peacefully and harmoniously in every way, which deserves the highest praise. I don't think I or any of those present will ever forget that occasion.

Since Ajaan Khao could not eat food, his condition steadily worsened. Meanwhile, more and more people kept pouring in from every direction. When I saw his condition begin to grow worse I began to stay with him regularly to help look after the situation. Only occasionally did I return to my own Wat for one or two nights before hurrying back to be with Ajaan Khao. I was very concerned about his health, but also I wanted to keep the atmosphere inside the Wat as peaceful and proper as possible. But the power of his great virtue (*pāramī*) looked after and protected the whole situation, maintaining peace and good behaviour.

When Ajaan Khao could no longer eat, his physical condition deteriorated rapidly, which was quite visible to everyone around him. When asked about how he was and whether he would depart from the world, he gave the most impressive exposition of the nature of his condition, saying:

"What is there to this body? When it dies, I'll feel no concerns and no regrets at all. All I can see in this body is a lot of earth, water, air and fire, which are the constituent elements that make up the physical aggregate. That's all there is. When the 'one who knows' — which is the heart — departs entirely, this body will immediately start to break down into its original elements of its own accord. If I were not concerned for the welfare of my Bhikkhu disciples and for the lay people who have come here, I would have no qualms at all about dying at this moment. I would then come to the end of all acknowledgement[11] and responsibility straightaway, so there would be no further burden for me to carry on my shoulders.

"The word Anālayo[12], which has been my name since my ordination, would then represent the truth, for the 'true-one' would arise then perfect and complete. At present my Anālayo is not perfect because the conventional aggregates (*sammuti khandha*), the five groups which form the body and mind (*pañcaka khandha*), require my attention, so I must take full responsibility for them. In other words, I must constantly direct them in living, in eating, in sleeping, in urinating, in excreting, and in changing bodily postures and moving about, like an electric fan spinning constantly round and round. Since when did *sammuti* (the relative world of supposition) ever become peaceful, still and satisfied? It's bound to whirl around all the time. Both the external world and the internal world are constantly whirling. How can we ever hope to gain happiness and harmony from things which are always whirling about? Anyone who hopes to gain happiness and harmony from these *khandhas*, which are a deep well of suffering and anxiety, will always be disappointed, for none of the *khandhas* will ever fulfil his desires. I have been carrying these *khandhas* about for eighty years already and I haven't seen anything truly satisfying coming from them. What stands out all the time is just *dukkha* — discontent — that's all; both minor discontent and major suffering, which in one way or another are there all the time. I've never seen calm and happiness arise in the *khandhas* in a way that I could experience it clearly. Even at normal times, when I don't have fever or sickness, *dukkha* still appears throughout the *khandhas*, such as the aches and pains occurring throughout the various parts of the body. I have never experienced pleasure (*sukha*) in the *khandhas*.

"What people like to call 'pleasure' is just a false concept, a common phrase that people like to use. In truth, this body and its various parts never clearly display anything pleasant for us to see. Instead, they only display the burden of suffering that we must bear — which can make us almost faint and die if the pain doesn't stop. We should not deceive ourselves about the *khandhas*, thinking that they will bring enough pleasure and happiness to please us. Instead, they are almost sure to bring endless suffering, which they load onto us so we have to carry it about wherever we go.

"I myself acknowledge that I have been dragging these burdensome *khandhas* around for eighty years already. How much longer will I have to go on shouldering this burden? What is left for me to search for that should make me want to carry about this load of fuel and fire with the view that these *khandhas* will bring me something wonderful? I have no doubts about these *khandhas*, both those which I am still living in and those which have broken up and gone in the past. I am I; the *khandhas* are the *khandhas*. What's the point of mixing them up together? Simply let go of the *khandhas* entirely — *anālayo* — then one is complete, as one should be.

"I freely admit that my heart is full of *mettā* and compassion for my fellow Bhikkhus and all the lay people. So, although I know that the *khandhas* are nothing but suffering, I can see the value of going on with this life for the sake of those people who need my help. For myself alone, I am always ready to let go of these *khandhas*, which indeed are a burden (*Bhārā have pañcakkhandhā*). They were truly a well full of tears for me when I used to covet them.

"But now I no longer covet them, I no longer worry about them, so I am prepared to release them to go naturally according to their basic nature. I shall not resist or oppose the truth. When I resisted the truth in the past, all I got was a lot of suffering, until I learnt to dread it. So this time I shall not resist, but instead let the *khandhas* go their natural way, which is the way of Dhamma — the unshakeable truth.

"Those who have accepted responsibility for rescuing themselves by way of the principles of nature were never compelled to do so by anyone. Rather, it was their own necessity that compelled them. Thus it is necessary for all of us to take responsibility for ourselves. We must not be negligent. We must accept that the *citta* is the fundamental basis that determines our way of living and all the good that we do. It also determines the characteristic modes of behaviour that we display externally, for which we must take responsibility by being constantly aware that we are the ones who do good and evil, so we must be responsible for our own external behaviour. In other words, we ourselves are the ones who receive the results of the good and evil of whatever work or actions we do. We know that the results of what we do are not lost anywhere, but that they will flow back to their original cause: we who did them in the first place.

"The 'we' I'm referring to here, which is the chief principle in people, means the 'heart'; and the heart does not die, nor has it ever died since the remotest antiquity. But it has gone astray, wandering about to become involved in birth, being born into all sorts of states both good and bad under the overriding influence of the results (*vipāka*) of the good and bad *kamma* which we have done.

"Especially important is the idea which some people have that after death there is just voidness, nothingness. This view is fundamentally wrong. The heart of the Lord Buddha and those of all the *Arahants* who have got rid of the *kilesas*, which would otherwise lead them into birth and death, have not been annihilated and reduced to nothing. They simply do not go wandering about searching for a place to be reborn; in contrast to the hearts of all others who have *kilesas*, which are the seeds that lead them to further birth and death. The hearts of the Lord Buddha and the *Arahants* are still their hearts, but they are in the state of *Nibbāna* without remainder (*Anupādisesa-nibbāna*) of those who have completely got rid of all their *kilesas*.

"There are various ideas such as: after death there is just nothingness; there is no such thing as evil; there is no such thing as merit; there is no such place as hell; there is no such place as heaven; there is no such state as *Nibbāna*. All of these are doctrines taught in the textbook of the *kilesas* that rule the Triple Universe. Having mastered these doctrines, the *kilesas* use them to govern the hearts of all living beings. No matter how severely they oppress living beings, they are not in the least afraid or concerned that anyone will dare to challenge their authority. Because their schooling is good and up-to-date, people accept it fully without reservations. All the knowledge that is learned from the textbook of the *kilesas* is bound to be knowledge which wipes out the truth of Dhamma. For example, the truth of Dhamma shows us that after death one is born again, whereas the knowledge which comes from the textbook of the *kilesas* teaches the opposite, that after death one is annihilated. In a similar way, Dhamma teaches that evil exists, merit exists, the hells exist, the heavens exist and *Nibbāna* exists, whereas the teaching of the *kilesas* immediately denies all of them by teaching that the opposite is true.

"This being so, we Buddhists must examine these matters thoroughly and choose well, otherwise we are likely to be overwhelmed by the teaching of the *kilesas*, which will lead us over the chasm and down towards the great *Avīci* hell. All because we are deceived into believing the tricks of the *kilesas* to the point where nobody can help us, since a birth in hell gives us no chance to remedy the situation. To remedy and wash clean the *kilesas* and their teaching that are buried deep in our hearts, we must do so by means of the Buddha-Dhamma, beginning now while we are still alive and the time is right. After we have died, the opportunity to do something about it will have passed. All that will be left then is the experiencing of the results of the good and evil actions we ourselves did as human beings.

"In the saying: *Attā hi attano nātho*[13], the Lord Buddha taught us to depend on ourselves, and not to expect to depend on anyone else in all the worlds of existence. He also taught that, from this moment onward, we should do good deeds for our own sake, which will make us feel comfortable and secure in our hearts for the rest of this life and after we die as well. We will then have Dhamma virtue to guard and protect us, which is very different from those who have little merit and little Dhamma in them. When they die, they are reborn in a realm which is disturbed and troubled accordingly. The *kilesas* that are *Māra* the enemy of Dhamma, must also be *Māra* the enemy of living beings everywhere, without a doubt. They show themselves by misleading beings and directing them only towards the fiery pit — which is the boundless mass of suffering where they find nothing that they can trust or hold onto as a refuge, even for a moment. The result is a combustible mixture of fuel and fire found in every nook and cranny, with no safe haven where beings can relax and breathe freely. The wisest of men in every age have always censured the *kilesas*; never have they claimed that the *kilesas* make the world a peaceful place, or that the *kilesas* are things which bring equality and justice to the world. They have always been full of tricks and deception in every age and era. They have never lost their ability to cheat and deceive beings in the world who are so stupid that they are to be pitied.

"On the other hand, Dhamma possesses the gentleness of love and compassion to help beings in the world to get free from ignorance, to get free from suffering and torment of all kinds. It supports their self-development, gives relief and alleviates their suffering so that they gain peace and happiness. The difference between the *kilesas* and Dhamma is so enormous that it is almost impossible to make comparisons. They are always working at cross-purposes. The *kilesas* are always deluding people, enslaving them and immersing them in the round of *dukkha*. Dhamma always gives support to people, drawing them up and out of the round of *dukkha* bit by bit, until they can reach *vimutti* — complete liberation. So, as you can see, there is a great difference between the *kilesas* and Dhamma."

I myself was the one who asked Ajaan Khao how he felt about his physical condition on that occasion. In response, he gave this powerful discourse, delivered in such a way that it appeared as though he had no serious illness, painful fever or weakness in his body at all. The way in which he spoke out quite startled those who were listening. The tone and tenor of his voice, his manner and appearance, and the intensity of the Dhamma flowing out from his pure heart all belied his physical condition. Nobody could have imagined that he would be able to defy his frail condition to deliver such a strong and forceful exposition on the nature of the *kilesas* and Dhamma. Those listening were all smiling and cheerful, their ears sharp and their eyes bright. But for myself, I'm the kind of character who is never satisfied, so I felt I could never hear enough of the Dhamma which he had kindly expounded. I wished to hear even more of it, so I squeezed in a special kind of Dhamma question at the end:

"Ajaan Khao, after this you will get better day by day until you are completely recovered. I have no doubt about this, because the Dhamma which you have kindly given us just now is the kind of Dhamma that burns out and cleanses diseases from the *khandhas*, so this illness is bound to break up and disperse. No kind of disease can withstand that kind of Dhamma. Even the *kilesas*, which are more robust and resistant than diseases, are bound to be destroyed by this powerful Dhamma."

Ajaan Khao answered in an impressive, unforgettable way that was wonderful to hear. He said:

"*Khandhas* are *khandhas*, sickness is sickness, *kilesas* are *kilesas*, Dhamma is Dhamma — each is of a different kind. Medicines are appropriate for treating and overcoming sickness. Dhamma is appropriate for counteracting and destroying *kilesas*, but it is unsuitable for overcoming some kinds of illness. There are forms of sickness which should be curable by means of Dhamma, and there are others which cannot be cured in that way. Those who practise the way should take good note of this. Don't let your ideas, your beliefs and your actions be in excess of what is right and reasonable.

"What I said today was pure Dhamma delivered for the purpose of arousing the joy of Dhamma in those listening, while also getting rid of their *kilesas*. It was not connected with the *khandhas* or with treating and curing this disease in the way you understand. It's not important whether the *khandhas* live or die. What is important is whether any *kilesas* died and left the heart of the listener due to the power of the Dhamma I expressed. That is truly the most appropriate result for those who practise the way of Dhamma. So we must use wisdom to examine and think about that Dhamma teaching, for it will encourage us to promote the methods of mindfulness and wisdom that enable us to continuously extract the *kilesas* that are within us.

"In the time of the Lord Buddha, they listened to Dhamma with *Opanayiko*[14] — steadily bringing the Dhamma which they heard into themselves — and didn't let it leak out and drift away, passing through their ears and hearts uselessly, which is how most of us listen to it nowadays. So the results of counteracting and uprooting the *kilesas* that we should expect to get while listening to Dhamma, hardly ever occur these days. In fact, people just as often accumulate *kilesas* while listening without being interested to consider whether they listen for the sake of Dhamma or for the sake of accumulating *kilesas*, which laugh at Dhamma.

"When the Lord Buddha or the *Sāvakas* gave a talk on Dhamma, what they said came from the pure and simple truth of Dhamma in their hearts. They didn't give talks based on what they had committed to memory like we do nowadays. Their practices and the way they went about doing things of all kinds, from the most ordinary to the most subtle, were all done to the best of their ability, with full knowledge of both the Path and its stages, as well as the Fruition in its various levels from the lowest up to the highest, which is *vimutti* — complete liberation. Their discourses, which were absolutely pure Dhamma, were given without any hesitation or uncertainty. This Dhamma poured out from the flow of the heart, blending in with the flow of the sound of their voices so that those who heard it with a sincere intention to realise the truth were able to help themselves to the true Dhamma to their heart's content. They never failed to gain some benefit from listening to

Dhamma. No matter how many *kilesas* there are, or how deeply ingrained they are, when mindfulness and wisdom shake them up and harass them without ceasing, the *kilesas* will be loosened up and uprooted bit by bit. In the end, the heart becomes an empty house void of all *kilesas*. Then the heart becomes filled with Dhamma in a way that is impossible to imagine.

"For that reason, we should make a determined effort to listen to Dhamma and to practise *bhāvanā* wholeheartedly. When we are sincere in the practice of Dhamma, then the *kilesas* will gradually be loosened up and uprooted without any doubt. This is as true now as it was at the time of the Lord Buddha. Those who practise the way truly are able to reach the Path, Fruition and *Nibbāna* in the same way as they used to then. This is what we should expect, for Dhamma is that 'nature' which is timeless and unchanging. The Middle Way of Practice, *Majjhima Paṭipadā*, has always been the most appropriate Dhamma for destroying the *kilesas* so that they vanish from the heart. There has never been anything more superior in any age. So guard against the *kilesas*, they are antagonistic to Dhamma. Don't let them climb up on your head, or else Dhamma will immediately lose out. You must be very careful.

"There! I've said enough to act as a timely reminder to those loyal devotees who have made the effort to come and visit me following the custom of those who have respect for their teacher."

VENERABLE AJAAN KHAO REMAINED SICK in the manner described above for more than four months. All the doctors who attended him, including Professor Ouay Ketasinh and several other doctors and nursing staff from Udon General Hospital, were instrumental in helping him to recover. They did everything possible to help him from the start, treating him to the best of their ability until his health returned to normal due to the skill of the doctors and those who looked after him. After his recovery, he seemed to have a new lease of life, as though a new person was there in the place of the old *ajaan*.

I must ask the reader to forgive me for dealing so briefly with Ajaan Khao's lengthy illness. I realise how inadequate a description this is of what actually took place. But I am also old now, my health is not so good and I'm kept busy dealing with a lot of different matters, which is like trying to keep up with the hoof prints of oxen inside a pen.

The Great Kilesa Family

One strange thing about Ajaan Khao was that when he thought about a certain animal, that animal tended to come to him. For example, he might think about an elephant that he knew and had not seen for a long time — maybe years — wondering if perhaps a hunter had shot and killed it. Then, in the middle of the night, that elephant would come looking for him and walk right up to the hut where he was staying and stand there. It gently played with some of the trees and plants nearby to let him know that it had come, after which it disappeared into the surrounding forest and never returned again. The same sort of thing happened when he wondered if a tiger that he had seen often in the past might have been killed. Having thought about that tiger in the middle of the day, that same night it came and roamed around the Wat where he was staying, before disappearing never to return again. He said that it was strange and unusual how whenever he thought about a specific animal, that same animal came looking for him almost every time. It was almost as if something went to tell them to pay him a visit. It seems likely that a Bhikkhu of such internal excellence as Ajaan Khao may have had a guardian *Deva* to watch over him and help him in various ways. At least, this is how many people believed it to be with Ajaan Khao, for whenever a thought of anything arose in him, it always seemed to illicit a response from the object of that thought. Otherwise, why should it come and search him out directly almost every time after the thought occurred to him?

As for the rest of us, we can think about such things time after time without receiving enough of a positive response to our thoughts and desires to let us know that we have the kind of superior virtue that Ajaan Khao possesses. Our thoughts tend to be so empty of real substance that they are more likely to trouble our hearts and make us suffer than anything else. Hardly anything truly good can be found in them at all. It's really disgraceful how our thoughts tend to bring us such a mass of *dukkha* every day that our brains become too dull and too weak to do any work.

VENERABLE AJAAN KHAO had a very resolute character; he always put forward great effort in doing the practice. He was very capable in walking *caṅkama*. Every day he used to walk in meditation from just after finishing his morning meal until

midday. Then he would rest to let his body recover before
sitting in *samādhi* for one or two hours. After that, he would
again return to the *caṅkama* path to do walking meditation. He
did not set a specific time, but would continue walking until it
was time to sweep the ground around the area where he was
staying, usually alone in a secluded place. After sweeping the
ground and taking a bath, he usually sat for awhile reflecting
on various aspects of Dhamma that intrigued him at that time.
Following that, he tended to prefer walking *caṅkama* to sitting
in *samādhi*. He walked for three to five hours, or sometimes
six hours, before resting for the night in what, during the dry
season, was usually no more than an open bamboo platform. In
the rainy season he would stay in a small thatched-roof hut that
was enough to give him protection from the elements without
being at all fancy. In fact, his hut would have appeared quite
inadequate and pitiful in the eyes of most people who are used
to the usual luxuries and amenities of life.

Before sitting to practise *samādhi bhāvanā*, he would
bow down and pay homage to a *Buddha Rūpa* and do some
chanting. He often chanted *suttas* for many hours at a time.
After finishing chanting, he then sat down in *samādhi bhāvanā*
and continued on for several hours before lying down to
have some sleep. When walking *caṅkama*, he walked for long
periods; when sitting in meditation, he sat for many hours at
a time; and when standing still, he often stood for a very long
time.[15] When necessary, he could stand still on his meditation
path and contemplate the meaning of Dhamma for hours until
he had cleared up all the questions that arose from the aspect
of Dhamma that he was investigating. Then he would go on
walking *caṅkama* as before. When he was younger, he often

sat in meditation continuously from dusk until dawn — though even then he was no longer a youth, for he ordained after the age of thirty years. But he was truly a warrior and a fighter on the path of Dhamma.

He often gave Dhamma talks to Bhikkhus which were strong and forceful. Often he would tell them:

"You must understand that the *kilesa* family which has ruled over the hearts of all living beings in the three worlds of existence for countless ages is very tough and tenacious. Its members are very powerful and extremely clever at using so many deceptive tricks to turn living beings upside down and inside out that it is almost impossible to describe all of their deceitful ways. The family of the *kilesas* is larger and more widespread than the heavens and the oceans, and all the territory of the three worlds is within the range of its techniques and its power, for it casts an influence over everything. There is nowhere, no nook or cranny — even the size of a grain of sand — where its ingenious techniques and tricky methods do not permeate. It pervades all things large and small: homes are full of it, towns are full of it, countries are full of it, the world is full of it and the whole universe is full of it. There is no corner anywhere where this *kilesa* family is not lying in wait ready to overpower living beings. The whole universe constitutes the kingdom ruled by the extended family of the *kilesas*. Their rule is so well-established that it is very difficult for anyone anywhere to escape from their iron grip. In fact, only the Lord Buddha and the *Arahants* have been able to do so. If you are still unfamiliar with the magic spells they use to hypnotize all living beings, then please learn about them here and now. You will gain mindfulness to warn you not to be complacent like you have been, and still are.

"What I have told you about the *kilesa* family comes from the indignation I felt for them at the time when I was struggling to defeat them. In the beginning, I was badly beaten by them. I often could not see any way to fight against them. But I would bounce back and attack them again each time. This went on in fits and starts, setting up mindfulness anew to fight them again time after time, only to lose out to them, back and forth continuously. As soon as I could raise my head again I would start to fight anew with the heart of a warrior, staking my life on the outcome. Fighting without retreating, I engaged the *kilesas* in battle while sitting, while walking and while standing. When I lay down, I would keep on battling them until I fell asleep. Every posture became a fighting posture. And although I lost out to them time after time, I never gave up, because I had yet to reach that point which I had determined to reach from the beginning, which was undisputed and complete victory. Only then could I stop fighting.

"When we fight and strive without drawing back or weakening, the strength and agility of our mindfulness and wisdom gradually grow and increase. The heart, which is used to being high-spirited and playful like a wild horse, can then gradually calm down. The heart, which up to this point has only memorised the meaning of *samādhi* as being 'firm and unshakeable calm', then gradually comes to experience *samādhi* as a firm and unshakeable calm arising within it. It then becomes quite clear that the *samādhi* which they wrote about in the ancient texts is true: it exists, it's real and it arises in the heart. When you have actually experienced *samādhi* in your own heart, all doubts about the *samādhi* described in the ancient texts will be cleared up. Then your heart will be peaceful and bright, open and free, where it had previously been so clogged up and constricted that your way forward had long been blocked.

"When this happened to me, it was an enlightening experience that led to the firm belief that I would surely be able to attain the Path, Fruition and *Nibbāna* in this lifetime. Just the calm experienced in *samādhi* was satisfying enough to make sure that I did not lack contentment in my life as a human being. The initial capital that I invested to amass the personal wealth which led to the Path, Fruition and *Nibbāna*, which I was certain I would attain one day, was the resource of *samādhi* — calm and peace of heart. Once I had attained this and seen it quite clearly, I was optimistic that by striving in the same way I could gradually gain greater and greater wealth in the practice of Dhamma.

"By that time, the four *Iddhipāda* were becoming apparent. These four are:

1. *Chanda* — a sense of satisfaction in the practice of meditation; and a sense of satisfaction in the results of meditation that arise in the heart continuously like spring water constantly seeping out of the ground, making the heart feel refreshed and happy all the time in all situations.

2. *Viriya* — ceaseless effort. All activities should be accompanied by the effort to eradicate the great family of *kilesas* and all its members.

3. *Citta* — a genuine interest in maintaining the wonderful taste of Dhamma within the heart at all times. Try to

make sure that no dangerous poisons penetrate to spoil the taste of Dhamma.

4. *Vimaṁsa* — internal contemplations and investigations that diligently search out and probe into causes and their results in connection with matters concerning the heart.

"We must try to train the *citta*, which the *kilesas* have rendered stupid, in order to improve it so that it grows and develops in the direction of Dhamma — which is the skilfulness of mindfulness and wisdom. Then the heart will not be down and confused like it was before. The four *Iddhipādas* will also gain increased strength day by day, causing the four factors of *chanda*, *viriya*, *citta* and *vimaṁsa* to blend together into one and so gain the power needed to confront the *kilesas* any time at any place, with the sole aim of destroying them completely.

"When *samādhi* has been developed enough to become well established within the heart, and can be set up at any time, you should then make haste to go in the direction of wisdom by investigating all *dhammas*[16], both internal and external, so they all converge into the *Ti-lakkhaṇa* — *annica*: impermanence, *dukkha*: discontent, *anattā*: void of any self essence. Then the four *Iddhipādas* begin to closely coordinate their work, until they become automatically functioning paths to power, following the lead of mindfulness and wisdom.

"From that point on, it would not be wrong to say that the struggle turns into hand-to-hand combat against the *kilesas*. Our fervent desire to gain freedom from *dukkha* gains strength with each passing moment, as we strive relentlessly for final liberation. If it means dying in the struggle, then let death come on the field of battle; in other words, let death come while fighting with the spirit of a warrior, just that! If death is avoided, then may the *kilesas* clearly succumb to the onslaught and fall dead all around every time they are attacked by those most up-to-date of weapons, mindfulness and wisdom.

"At the beginning of meditation practice, before the *citta* attains a calm state of *samādhi*, even the meditator who strives boldly, putting his life on the line, will tend to end up badly 'bruised'. The results that he gets will not seem commensurate with the effort he makes. This is because he is still not as skilled at fighting the *kilesas* as he should be. So it is necessary for someone who practices the way to accept the fact that he will be subjected to quite a lot of 'bruising' to begin with. Through experience he begins to understand the reasons for this, and he learns to adjust the nature of his effort and the methods that he uses to make them more suitable in the future. I've been through the same kind of experience myself. I nearly died before I was able to grasp the principles of meditation properly.

"When the practice for the development of wisdom dissects the body into its various parts, separating them out and examining them in terms of their true nature as being loathsome (*asubha*), unsatisfactory (*dukkha*), impermanent (*annica*) and without self-identity (*anattā*), until these truths gradually become quite clear, then our efforts at striving can be said to have 'taken off' and become bold and venturesome. The results will be evident in the development of mindfulness and wisdom, which step out to work in the field of the five *kammaṭṭhānas* − hair of the head (*kesā*), hair of the body (*loma*), nails (*nakhā*), teeth (*danta*) and skin (*taco*), right through to the nature of phenomena (*sabhāva-dhamma*) everywhere. This is done with rapt attention to the examination, which allows us to see the truth of the physical body and its various parts until it has gone throughout every part and linked up with external phenomena such as exist everywhere — at which point we see that they are all of the same kind. This gets rid of all doubts and uncertainties about the body and leads steadily to the breaking of all attachment to it.

"The type of mindfulness and wisdom used to examine and analyse the physical body is very bold and venturesome, in fact, more so than that normally used in other areas of meditation. But it is appropriate to the task at hand — which is quite gross and needs bold and venturesome mindfulness and wisdom to succeed. It's rather like an untrimmed lump of wood that requires heavy-handed methods to get it into shape. In a similar way, the mindfulness and wisdom used to examine the nature of the body, which is the grossest aspect of the *khandhas*, must act in accordance with what is appropriate to the task at hand. When mindfulness and wisdom finally know this *khandha* as it should be known and all attachment to it is broken, the examination will drop away of itself. It is similar to the work of a skilled carpenter who shapes up a piece of wood in whatever way he deems necessary. When a skilled carpenter who is shaping up a piece of wood reaches the stage where all the rough work is finished, he simply stops doing that kind of work without the need for anyone to tell him when to stop.

"The mental *khandhas*, which include: feeling (*vedanā*), memory (*saññā*), thought and imagination (*sankhāra*) and consciousness (*viññāṇa*), are more subtle *khandhas*. So the way that wisdom investigates them must also be correspondingly more subtle. The mindfulness and wisdom used to examine these four *khandhas* must exhibit a refined and subtle nature, much like water that permeates everywhere. The examination of the four mental *khandhas* leads directly to the *Ti-lakkhaṇa*. Any one of the three (*annica*, *dukkha* or *anattā*) may be used, depending on which one is the easiest to use in the investigation. But there is no scope for using the method of seeing loathsomeness (*asubha*) as there was when examining the body — which is the gross *khandha*.

"Any one of the four mental *khandhas* may be chosen for investigation. For instance, the *vedanā khandha* in which painful feeling occurs. There you must examine the relationship between the body, the *citta* and the painful feeling. Separate these factors out, and compare the nature of the physical body with the nature of feeling to find out what is what. Are these one and the same thing, or are they each of a different kind? Look at them, analyse them and see them clearly with true wisdom. Don't merely go over them half-heartedly and then pass on — which is the way the *kilesas* do work, by bringing up laziness and feebleness to defeat us. This is not the way to progress in Dhamma, for Dhamma means going forward with true mindfulness and wisdom. You will never get to see the truth in any other way. You must investigate in the pattern of mindfulness and wisdom, until you fully understand the truth in every case.

"When investigating painful feeling, don't wish for the pain to go away, because the more you want to get rid of it, the more you increase the Cause of *Dukkha*, the factor that creates more and more suffering. Rather, you should desire to know and understand the truth of painful feeling that displays itself in the body and in the heart. This kind of desire is the Path (*Magga*) on which you trample all over the *kilesas*, which in turn gives rise to the Fruition of the Path (*Phala*) when you see the truth about bodily feeling very clearly. The more the *citta* doing the investigation desires to know and understand the truth at that time, the more its efforts to that end will increase in strength.

"So, when investigating painful feeling, you should be interested only in gaining insight into the true nature of pain, while at the same time pushing any desire to get rid of the pain out from the field of that investigation. Don't let a desire for the pain's disappearance obstruct your progress, otherwise that negative desire will destroy the positive desire for the Path and its Fruition without you being aware of it. Then you will fail to find what you are looking for. Instead, you will meet with only the fear of death, and a weak attitude that seeks dependence on other people. This is a matter of the *kilesas*, the causes of *dukkha*, doing their work in the field of your striving. That's why I'm in a hurry to warn all of you who practice meditation, fearing that otherwise the *kilesas* will make a fool of you. The *kilesas* tend to move too fast for us to keep up and see through them. Only those who practice *citta bhāvanā* will be able to clearly understand the deceptive tricks of the various *kilesas*, and then drive them all out from their hearts completely.

"When examining painful feeling in the *khandhas*, especially in the body, don't think about the severity of the pain or its possible consequences for your health. Instead, think about realising the true nature of the body, the feeling and the *citta*. All three of them are ready to display the truth to those practising the way with the boldness of a warrior who settles for nothing less than a clear and comprehensive understanding of the Buddha's Noble Truths.

"The fear that causes us to want the pain to go away is the commander in chief of the *kilesa* family, which saps our energy and reduces our strength to resist until nothing is left. Please be aware and keep firmly in mind that we must not be deluded by his tricks, for he is waiting in ambush at the entrance to the path, ready to block our way and oppose our progress in Dhamma whenever there is a chance for us to go forward. Keep in mind that none of the *kilesas* are ever weak, or careless or clumsy in the same way that those who practice *bhāvanā* tend to be. We tend to simply roll over and allow the *kilesas* to drag us off and pound us to mincemeat, then cook us up as a tasty treat for the whole family.

"So, when you reach a crucial point in the battle between strong painful feeling and the mindfulness and wisdom that is investigating and analysing them so as to reach the truth, you must turn your mindfulness and wisdom to confront and to penetrate the pain. In other words, mindfulness and wisdom spin around and go down to that point in the body where the pain seems to be most severe. Mindfulness focuses the mind as wisdom disentangles the feeling, the body and the *citta*, which are all mixed up together, to find out whether these three are one and the same thing, or three separate entities. Analyse the situation between the body, the feeling and the *citta*, looking at them in precise detail, going back and forth and reviewing them over and over again with mindfulness and wisdom. Don't be concerned about the severity of the pain, whether it will disappear or whether you will live or die, or anything else, like the place where you're staying or the time of day. At that time you must be concerned only about the investigation you are doing to realise clearly the true nature of the body, the feeling and the *citta*, and nothing else. Mindfulness and wisdom must constantly keep the mind in the present moment and take precise and detailed note of the work that's being done. Don't allow the mind to deviate from the task at hand. Don't expect any particular result and don't speculate about the nature of the cause of *dukkha*, the path leading to its cessation, or its cessation, assuming that they must be like this or like that. All such thoughts merely open a door for the cause of *dukkha* to get in and do its work in the sphere of your efforts to practise the way. They do nothing but increase the amount of suffering you experience.

"Those of us who practise the way must constantly be very wary of the *kilesas*, so we cannot afford to relax and lose focus. At the same time, we should set our minds to do the investigation I've described, approaching it as though it were hand-to-hand combat. Whatever is good will survive to unite with the truth of Dhamma that is the true nature of freedom; whatever is bad will be destroyed. But don't let yourself be overwhelmed and destroyed in the struggle. You must battle courageously so that only the *kilesas* are destroyed. Any other result would be wrong and inappropriate for someone who practises the way like a warrior in battle who is determined to win unconditionally.

"When examining bodily pain in conjunction with the *citta*, you should separate it into three categories to realise its true nature by relentlessly using wisdom. Then you will come to know the truth of the body, the pain and the *citta* quite clearly without any doubt remaining, which will gradually, one battle at a time, lead you to victory over the *kilesas*. Not only will you become fearless in the face of severe pain, but you will also be fearless in the face of death, which will be seen as a natural truth in the same way as the body, the feeling and the *citta*. Then you will gain freedom from the fear of death, which is one of the great deceits that the *kilesas* have perpetrated to delude us.

"Once the truth of them is clearly understood, each is seen to be true in its own sphere. The body is true in accordance with the conditions that apply to the body, the feeling is true in accordance with the conditions that apply to the feeling, and the *citta* is true in accordance with the conditions that apply to the *citta*. Each of them is true in its own way without influencing or disturbing the others. Even death is a true natural principle, so why get so shaken up about it and give the *kilesas* a reason to laugh at you?

"When mindfulness and wisdom investigate without retreating until they understand clearly the truth of the body, the feeling and the *citta*, one of several things happens:

1. All painful feeling vanishes in an instant at that moment.

2. Even if the pain does not disappear, it does not make contact with the *citta* as it used to.

3. The *citta* becomes profoundly calm and wonderful beyond belief.

4. The *citta* which has become calm manifests an amazing state of 'just knowing'[17], and nothing else is associated with it.

5. While the *citta* is fully in this state of calm, the body disappears entirely from awareness.

6. If the *citta* has investigated thoroughly until it has severed its connection with the pain, but has not become fully integrated and dropped into a state of oneness, it simply knows everything all around; while the body simply exists without any direct connection to the *citta*.

"These are the results that come from the investigative methods I have described. They are only found within the circle of practice. If you want to experience these results for yourself, you must practise following the methods outlined above. Then the explanations you have read will surely come true in your own practice.

"The remaining three mental groups (*nāma khandhas*), which include memory, thought construction and consciousness, are sometimes investigated in connection with the body in the same way as feeling. This point has been brought up for those who do the practice to think about and investigate on their own according to the circumstances that arise in their meditation. After the *citta* has seen into and let go of the *rūpa khandha* completely, the investigation of these three *nāma khandhas* becomes the main task. But as long as the *citta* still has not let go of the *rūpa khandha*, the investigation is bound to be inextricably linked with the physical body. It is the duty of each individual meditator to know this for himself.

He may know within himself that he should do an investigation that covers all the *khandhas*, or that he should focus on one particular *khandha*. Only the meditator himself will understand which investigations will be most conducive to letting go of his attachment to the *khandhas* at each level of practice.

"The *rūpa khandha* requires a very broad, sweeping kind of investigation. The human body is a very extensive and complex subject, so techniques used in the investigation cannot be fixed; they must be flexible. It depends on the individual to devise his own methods. You can mentally dissect the human body into its constituent parts, until all that remains is pieces where previously there was a person. You can investigate to see the body's repulsive nature (*asubha*), focusing on its disgusting aspects. You can investigate the body in terms of any one of the *Ti-lakkaṇa* (*annica*, *dukkha* and *anattā*), or in terms of all three of them together. You should go on doing this until the *citta* becomes skilled and adept in both the field of *asubha* and in the field of the *Ti-lakkaṇa*, and further until all doubts have been alleviated. Then letting go of your attachment to the body will take place automatically on its own.

"When the *citta* has let go of the *rūpa khandha*, it will turn its attention to the three *nāma khandhas*, which are memory, thought formations and consciousness, pursuing them relentlessly with the absolute maximum of whatever mindfulness and wisdom it has. Because they are already at the stage of being fully proficient, mindfulness and wisdom will go about this work on their own without having to be in any way forced to do so. This adeptness of mindfulness and wisdom began displaying itself at the stage when the investigation of loathsomeness in

201

the body was practised. By the time the body had been completely let go of, this proficiency was already fully developed.

"When the *citta* then turns its attention to memory, thought formations and consciousness, it is already skilled and fully proficient at investigating into every corner and from all angles. The *citta* no longer shows any signs of sluggishness and apathy; rather, its incessant activity must be restrained when it becomes so absorbed in the investigation that it does not want to take a rest — which means resting in *samādhi*. At this stage, the terms *mahā-sati* and *mahā-paññā* that we have read about in the ancient texts will come to life in the mindfulness and wisdom that revolves ceaselessly around the *nāma khandhas*, investigating each and every aspect of them. There is no need to ask anyone else about it.

"From the point where the true nature of *asubha* is realised quite clearly by means of investigation, all laziness and weariness disappear entirely. They seem to be completely absent from the *citta*. For this reason, it becomes obvious that laziness and indifference are both just members of the *kilesa* family. They bind the legs and bind the hearts of living beings all the time so that they cannot step onto the path towards what is good and right.

"But as soon as they are torched by the ascetic fire of Dhamma (*tapa dhamma*), led by mindfulness and wisdom, they are burned to destruction. After that, laziness never appears in the *citta* again. All that remains is an intense concentration on all aspects of striving the whole time, except only in sleep. Even though the *kilesas* are still lurking in the heart, they don't dare to obstruct one's efforts in meditation. Then it's only a matter of time before the *kilesas* are laid to rest for good. An investigation of the three *nāma khandhas*, done by someone who has already developed superior mindfulness and wisdom when dealing with the *rūpa khandha*, will progress both quickly and proficiently. No other level of mindfulness and wisdom anywhere in the relative world of convention acts so quickly.

"The *citta* which has already let go of the *rūpa khandha* still has to train mindfulness and wisdom using the visual images of the physical body that arise in the thinking mind as their object. Mindfulness and wisdom track these images as they constantly arise and then cease, arise and cease, time after time until the images of the body appear and disappear as quickly as flashes of lightning. After that, the *citta* becomes empty of all bodily forms, and empty of all material forms, both external and internal. All interest in investigating these things dies away from then on.

"The mind's full attention then turns to examine one or the other of the three *nāma khandhas*, or all three of them together at the same time. Since all three of these mental factors arise in the *citta* and cease in the *citta*, the *citta* itself now becomes the main target of the investigation. These conditions of the *citta* are observed as they arise and cease and are probed into with wisdom. When mindfulness and wisdom finally penetrate to the true nature of these *khandhas*, memory, thought and consciousness are seen to be transitory phenomena that continually appear and disappear without any actual continuity.

"The *citta* at this stage of investigating the *nāma khandas* is empty of everything from the external world. But it is still not empty of the three mental *khandhas*. So the *citta* must scrutinize all three carefully, seeing them as *anicca*, *dukkha* and *anattā* time and time again until the *citta* is satisfied about the nature of the *khandhas*. Then all that remains is the *citta* on its own, which is the exclusive home of *avijjā* (fundamental ignorance). The investigation continues to focus on the association between the *citta* and the *nāma khandhas* until mindfulness and wisdom clearly understand the harmfulness and deceit of the *nāma khandhas* together with *avijjā*. Then the *avijjā* in the *citta* disintegrates, completely disappearing from the heart at that moment.

"When *avijjā*—which is the essence of the *kilesas*—vanishes from the *citta*, the *khandhas*—which are the tools of the *kilesas* and *avijjā*—do not disappear along with *avijjā*. Instead, they turn into tools of the pure *citta*, continuing on as undefiled *khandhas* without any *kilesas* getting in and taking charge as they used to. The pure *citta* and the pure Dhamma do not coerce the *khandhas* or cling to them in the way the *kilesas* did. The *citta* merely relies on the *khandhas* as its instruments in an impartial way.

"This is the work of cleansing the charnel grounds of birth and death from the heart so that they completely cease to exist. The wisest of people always cleanse themselves in this way. Please remember this well and strive to put it into practice so that all of you may realise the nature of the true Dhamma. At the moment the *citta* realises that Dhamma is pure throughout, it will also realise the true nature of all the Buddhas. Then all doubts about the true nature of the Lord Buddha, the Dhamma and the Sangha will vanish as well.

"The war between the *kilesas* and Dhamma that was waged on the battlefield of the heart then stops right there in the heart of the meditator, which becomes completely pure after the *kilesas* are destroyed and disappear. At that point, all problems cease. So I implore my followers, both Bhikkhus and others, to get to know the Dhamma that shakes the world and wakes up all beings from the sleep of the *kilesas*. Get to know it right now while there are *ajaans* still teaching the way. Then you won't continually fall prey to the *kilesas* like you have in the past, which is a pitiful sight in the eyes of those wise men who are far more clever than the *kilesas* in every way. We who are lulled to sleep by the *kilesas* even while we are still awake are likely to see what is worthless as being valuable. We tend to see what is harmful as being good and what is meritorious as being evil. The heavy burden we bear is worn as a beautiful, shiny ornament that gives us great satisfaction. When we try to do something virtuous, we tend to do it casually in a careless manner, just going through the motions, so the results are hit-and-miss. We can't find any consistency or standard that we can rely on. Like a stick stuck into a pile of buffalo shit that's just waiting to fall over, we can never find any firm ground in ourselves. All that's left is a heart lacking any essential meaning, so all of our actions tend to be harmful to us. This happens because we neglect to train our habitual tendencies to act in the ways which are right and proper.

Because of this neglect, Bhikkhus become worthless monks and lay people become worthless persons. They are scattered among the good people of this world, whom they greatly outnumber. If we are to choose between the righteous and true Bhikkhus who are 'practising in the right way' (*supaṭipatti*) — or the righteous and true lay followers who are practising *dāna*, *sīla* and *bhāvanā* — and the worthless Bhikkhus and lay people, which path will we choose? We must examine this matter well and decide quickly, for once we are dead, it will be too late. The virtue that we should expect to gain does not come simply from wearing the yellow robes, or from inviting Bhikkhus to chant the *kusala-mātikā* and accept *paṁsukūla* robes at our funeral. It depends solely on us training ourselves to have *kusala dhamma* — which means to be skilled at removing all bad things from our hearts while we are still alive. Don't say I didn't warn you!

"Please take note of this warning and remember it in your hearts; then always try to put it into practise by following the way of *attā hi attano nātho* — always try to rely on yourself as you walk the path, allowing Dhamma to light the way. Then you won't be an old-fashioned Bhikkhu or an old-fashioned lay person, behind the times in regard to goodness and virtue and the Path, Fruition and *Nibbāna* which the Lord Buddha taught in a fresh, contemporary manner with supreme *mettā*.

"I myself am growing older and older every day, and it is no longer easy for me to lead and teach my followers. Meanwhile, Bhikkhus and novices keep flooding into the monastery in larger and larger numbers to receive training and teaching. When you come to study and train with me, you must commit yourselves to the practice with real determination. Don't bring along a half-hearted attitude, damaging yourself and your friends who have set their hearts on the practice of Dhamma, for this will ruin both you and the others.

"The *kilesas* do not spare anyone, no matter who they are. We Bhikkhus and novices must understand that the *kilesas* have always been our enemies. They are not afraid of anybody, even monks. You must not think that they will bow down and offer their services to you, attending on you and taking care that all the conditions for meditation practice are comfortable and convenient so that you, their great teacher, will not be troubled in any way. Although you have been ordained as a Bhikkhu, the basic nature of the *kilesas* in your heart has not changed — they have been squatting on your head since long before you ordained, and they will never agree to come down on their own. Because they have always been tyrants which bully Bhikkhus and lay people alike, they are not afraid of anyone anywhere in the world. And they will continue in this way endlessly if you don't hurry to get rid of them completely from this moment on, so that they are utterly destroyed and dispelled from the heart.

"Today I have opened my heart and explained to you everything I know about the path of practice. I have described the causes, which are the rigorous methods that are effective for fighting the *kilesas*; and the effects, which are the various results brought about by diligently following these methods. All of these I have disclosed to you without holding anything back. Nothing, however small, has been left hidden or concealed.

"So now each of you should take these methods and use them to the best of your ability to straighten out the onerous, unruly *kilesas* within yourselves. But be careful not to let the *kilesas* straighten you out — by making you lie prostrate before them — instead of you straightening them out. This is something which concerns me greatly, so I don't want to see it happen to you. I myself have been flattened by them in the past. I learned such a powerful lesson from it that I cannot help but warn all of you to avoid the same pitfall."

VENERABLE AJAAN KHAO'S LIFE AND PRACTICE is a truly amazing story. It clearly illustrates the Dhamma teaching about the effectiveness of stubborn determination and anger when directed against one's own *kilesas*. He was strongly imbued with both of these factors in his practice of Dhamma. Ajaan Khao possessed a remarkably resolute character and liked to put his whole strength into whatever he did. He had been like that since he was a lay person, and when he was ordained he carried these characteristics over with him. The longer he was ordained in Buddhism, which is a true religion that teaches people to act truly in whatever they do, the more he felt impressed by the principles of Dhamma.

Both Ajaan Khao's mode of practice and his level of spiritual attainment are worthy of the utmost respect. He always preferred to practice in remote, secluded locations with such single-minded resolve that his diligence in this respect was unrivalled among his peers in the circle of *Dhutanga Bhikkhus*.

Ajaan Khao had a streak of very strong determination in his character, which may be seen from what has been written about him. He had no difficulty in sitting in meditation from dusk until dawn — he could sit all night whenever he chose to do so. Sitting in meditation practice from dusk to dawn is no small matter. Unless one is the kind of person who has a heart so full of courageous determination that it could cut through a diamond, one cannot do it. So we should give him our heartfelt praise and admiration. In ways such as this he was fully capable of being an inspiration to his disciples, enabling them to gain peace and happiness by following faithfully in his footsteps. When he was alive and still possessed the five *khandhas*, he had absolute certainty in himself that he had reached the end of becoming and birth — this was completely self-evident to him. When it came time for him to let go of the *khandhas*, he attained the state of ultimate happiness *(Paramaṁ Sukhaṁ)* in all respects, totally free of all responsibilities and concerns.

May good fortune and blessings come to all of you who read the biography of this truly amazing spiritual warrior. As long as you do not give up your striving in the practice which leads to Dhamma, one day you will surely admire the pure treasure of Dhamma to your complete satisfaction, just as Ajaan Khao has in his own heart. This is bound to be the case, for Dhamma belongs to everybody who practises in the Right Way.

Ajaan Khao passed away on the 16th of May, 1983. He was 94 years old, and had been a monk for 64 years.

Epilogue

Nibbāna is inherent within the realm of human existence, but it is not something specifically human. *Nibbāna* cannot be found in the elements of earth, water, fire or air, or in anything of the physical world. Figuratively, we may say that *Nibbāna* is a place of absolute freedom; but, in truth, *Nibbāna* is a natural principle inherent within all of us. It has no physical characteristics whatsoever. The five senses cannot know it; philosophy cannot reveal it; science cannot verify it. Even extensive study of the Buddha's teaching cannot reach *Nibbāna* unless the teaching is diligently put into practice. Only by practising Buddhist meditation can the heart make the adjustments needed to realise *Nibbāna*. All of the many past Buddhas and their countless *Arahant* disciples did just that, allowing the truth arise unequivocally within their hearts.

So if you want to resolve doubts about the ultimate consequences of your actions, you must resolve them internally by practising meditation until you clearly realise the truth of these things for yourself. Even doubts that have plagued you for your whole life will dissipate in a flash at the moment that realisation occurs — even perpetual darkness turns to brightness the moment a light is turned on.

The truth of the Buddha's teaching will be revealed to those who truly practise his teaching with diligence and an unwavering determination to discover the truth. In order to fully realise the truth about their own nature and about the nature of Dhamma, seekers of the way must strive to become spiritual warriors on the path to liberation. Their hearts need to have a firm resolve that can boldly stand up to their internal enemies, finding the strength of will to fight with all their might without becoming weak or disheartened, and without retreating when the struggle becomes difficult. When this kind of fighting spirit is exhibited in the pursuit of Dhamma, then time and place are not relevant to their quest for the truth. Regardless of whether it is the Buddha's age or our present age, *Nibbāna* can always be attained by those who earnestly follow the way with diligence, because the true Dhamma always exists in the present moment — the timeless present, here and now.

Appendix

The Five Khandhas

The Five *Khandhas* consist of the aggregates of body, feeling, memory, thought and imagination, and consciousness. It is difficult to appreciate the depth and subtlety of meaning within these five groups, so in order to give the reader some basis for contemplation, a list of similes is given. These similes were taught by the Buddha. They may be found in the section on the *Khandhas* in the *Saṁyutta Nikāya*.

1. The body is likened to a lump of foam floating down the river Ganges.
2. Feeling is likened to rain falling into a puddle of water. As each raindrop falls, it causes a splash and a bubble which quickly bursts and disappears.
3. Memory is likened to a mirage seen in the desert. It has no substance to it; it is merely appearance.
4. Thought and imaginative thinking are likened to a plantain tree. When the outer layers of the trunk are peeled off, no substantial pith or hardwood is found inside.

> 5. Consciousness is likened to a magician who stands at the crossroads and displays all sorts of magical illusions, which are devoid of any real substance.

When talking about the *nāma khandhas* (mental groups), we tend to think of them as being separate things or entities; but, in fact, they are all aspects of the *citta*. It is therefore more correct to think in terms of the *citta* performing the functions of feeling, memory, thought or consciousness; for all of them are thoroughly dynamic, and so not static entities at all.

Memory (Saññā)

It has become popular to translate the Pāli word *saññā* as "perception", but this is a wrong translation. It seems probable that this misunderstanding stems from translations of parts of the *Ti-piṭaka* carried out in the late 19th and early 20th centuries by scholars who tried to fit Buddhist ideas into Western philosophical concepts. The Concise Oxford Dictionary defines "perceive" as, 'to apprehend with the mind, observe, understand; to apprehend through one of the senses'. And "perception" is defined as, 'act, faculty of perceiving; intuitive recognition; (philos.) action by which the mind refers its sensations to external object as cause'.

The above definitions refer to complex processes that involve all of the mental *khandhas*, not just one. One function of the mental *khandhas* that has been ignored is 'memory'. If *saññā* is not translated as memory, then where is memory in the *khandhas*? Throughout Thailand, *saññā* is always translated by

214

"kwam chum", which means memory. This is universally accepted by both scholars and those who practice meditation.

Not enough thought has been given to the overwhelming importance of memory. Surely this should be clear to anyone who understands the devastating effect of Alzheimer's disease in which the memory steadily diminishes until the unfortunate victim has no reference left from past experience and he becomes virtually an imbecile.

The Ascetic Practices (Dhutangas)

The *Dhutangas* are ascetic practices that Buddhist monks voluntarily undertake. It must be understood that their purpose in every case is to counteract specific defilements (*kilesa*). So they are to be applied by each practitioner as and when he finds need for them.

1. Wearing robes that are patched and mended.
2. Wearing only the three principal robes and no others.
3. Getting ones food by going on the alms round.
4. Not omitting any house on the alms round.
5. Eating food only once a day, at one sitting.
6. Eating only out of the alms bowl.
7. Refusing to accept food offered after the alms round.
8. Living in the forest.
9. Living under a tree.
10. Living in the open; not at the foot of a tree, nor under a roof.
11. Living in a charnel ground.

12. Being satisfied with any available bed or resting place.
13. The sitter's practice; in other words, sitting, standing or walking, but never lying down.

Ārammaṇa

The word '*ārammaṇa*' means: a foundation, a support or that on which something depends. But generally speaking, in this book, this 'something' refers to the state of mind and what flows out of it. As a supporting condition for mental states, the *ārammaṇa* may be an externally sensed object or an internal condition arising from feeling, memory, thought or consciousness.

Amongst those who practice the way of *kammaṭṭhāna*, the word *ārammaṇa* is often used to refer to an emotional mental state, either good or bad; although, to be strictly correct, it should refer to that which arouses or precipitates that mental state.

In the Thai language, the word *ārammaṇa*, pronounced "arom", always means 'the emotions' in general. Sometimes in this book it also means the emotions.

NOTES

Path One — Buddha Pūjā

1. That Phanom is a well known Chetiya on the bank of the Mekong River in Nakon Phanom province.

2. Klod. A large monk's umbrella hung up on any suitable support. A cylindrical mosquito net usually hangs down from the edge of the klod to give protection from insects and, to some extent, wind and rain.

3. The one *citta* is the same as the one Dhamma in which all duality has dropped away.

4. *Āsava* is generally divided into four categories: 1) *Kāmāsava*: sensual desires; 2) *Bhavāsava*: the desire for existence; 3) *Diṭṭhāsava*: views and opinions; 4) *Avijjāsava*: ignorance. *Āsava* is usually translated as "cankers" or "corruptions" — although etymology suggests that "outflows" would be the best translation.

5. *Tapa Dhamma*. Ascetic fire. *Tapa* is thought of as being like a bright fire that burns up the *kilesas*.

6. *Nirodha* means the Cessation of *Dukkha*. *Nirodha* and *Magga* (the Path leading to the Cessation of *Dukkha*) are the third and fourth of the Four Noble Truths.

7. The base level or the basic foundation of the heart.

8. In other words, feelings are phenomena that exist in accordance with the true nature of feeling. The *citta* is also true in accordance

with its natural state of knowing. Each of them exists separately in their own natural spheres.

9. *Vihāra-dhamma* means dwelling in and with Dhamma. In other words, Dhamma is constantly present in the *citta* in terms of thought, contemplation and attitude.

10. One wall of the hut hinged at the top so that it swings out and up to let in more air. Such huts are usually made of split bamboo and straw.

Path Two — Dhamma Pūjā

1. *Rāga* usually refers to lust or sexual excitement, but can have a wider connotation also.

2. The attainment of the cessation of feeling and memory is the temporary suspension of all consciousness and mental activity.

3. In Thai, the normal word for to lie down is "norn". But for a Bhikkhu there is a special word "chum-wad". To distinguish the difference I have used the phrase 'to lie down properly' for the latter word.

4. *Dhammānudhamma.*

5. *Nimitta* is a form of mental perception which is usually visual, but may occur in terms of any of the senses. It is somewhat like a dream image, but usually appears starkly clear and often in a normal state of consciousness, so that the *nimitta* may appear to be a physical object in the world. They arise from various causes which are usually internal, but can be external as well.

6. Literally: "… one who has a single time…" In other words, all times are the same in the present.

Path Three — Sangha Pūjā

1. The drum was shaped like an elongated barrel, a type common in Southeast Asia. The cave might more properly be called "cave of the drum used to announce that it is time for the midday meal."

2. Boon Nah literally means "great or much merit", and Nai Baap Nah means "Master Great Evil".

3. This is only a way of speaking, for the hunter was most probably not a relative of the old man.

4. *Yakkha* is a demon or ogre, often with a cruel and murderous temperament.

5. *Sandiṭṭhiko.* Lit: "seeing for oneself".

6. The *Paṭimokkha* is the set of 227 rules which form a Bhikkhu's basic code of discipline.

7. This may be compared with an army officer who has decorations to display his status.

8. The requisites of a Bhikkhu being robe-cloth, food, shelter and medicine.

9. The winnowing basket is like a circular sieve. The meaning is that just as the ant just goes round and round the edge not knowing how to get off, so too do living beings go round and round the cycle of rebirth without knowing how to escape.

10. Astringent olive-like fruits that are eaten as medicines.

11. Acknowledgement (lit: receive/know), refers to the acknowledgement of sensation via the six senses, and of meaning and relationship.

12. *Anālayo* means "free from desires", "free from attachment". It is synonymous with *Nibbāna*.

13. *Attā hi attano nātho*: Let self be the refuge of self.

14. *Opanayiko* means "leading to" or "bringing near".

15. Usually, standing meditation occurs while one is on the *caṅkama* path. In other words, he would be walking when something arose that needed to be thought out. He would then stop and stand to work it out. After he understood it clearly he would begin walking as before.

16. The word *dhammas*, in this case, means practically everything that one can know. A possible translation might be "data".

17. This is a pure state of knowing without any delusion of subject-object.

GLOSSARY

Ācariya	Teacher. Sometimes also a term of respect for a senior Bhikkhu.
Anālayo	Free from desires; free from attachment. It is synonymous with *Nibbāna*.
Arahant	One who is worthy, one who attains the ultimate state of *Nibbāna*.
Ārammaṇa	Support; a supporting condition for the mind; an object.
Āsava	Outflows; that is, the *citta* flows out into sense desires, into perpetuating existence, into views and opinions, and into ignorance.
Avijjā	Fundamental ignorance; ignorance of one's own true nature.
Āyatana	Sense fields; that is, the fields of seeing, hearing, etc.; mental sensation.
Bhāvanā	Development by means of meditation.
Bhikkhu	A monk, usually in reference to Buddhism; one who lives on donated food.
Caṅkama	Walking meditation; pacing back and forth on a path designed for meditation.
Citta	The underlying essence of mind where Dhamma and the *kilesas* dwell. In its pure state it is indefinable. It is beyond birth and death. It controls the *khandhas*, but does not die when they do.
Deva	An angel-like being of the *Deva*-realms, which are immediately above the human realm.

Glossary

Dhamma	Truth; the ultimate order underlying everything; the teaching of the Buddha.
Dhammā(s)	In the plural, means: objects of mind, concepts, theories.
Dhutanga	Ascetic practices. See Appendix.
Dukkha	Discontent, suffering.
Iddhipāda	Roads to Power.
Indriya	Faculty, function.
Kamma	Lit: "action". In Buddhism, action of the body, speech or mind which has a moral content of good, bad or neutral. Such action brings back a corresponding result.
Kammaṭṭhāna	Lit: "basis of work"; refers to the "occupation" of a practising Bhikkhu.
Khandha	A heap or group. Usually refers to the Five *Khandhas*: the physical body, feeling, memory, thought and imagination, and consciousness.
Kilesa	The mental defilements based upon greed, hate and delusion.
Magga	Path; usually refers to the eight-fold path leading to *Nibbāna*.
Māra	The evil one; the personification of evil and temptation.
Mettā	Friendliness; pure love.
Nāma	Mental phenomena; the four mental factors of the Five *Khandhas*.
Nibbāna	Lit: "Extinguished"; the ultimate goal of Buddhist training.
Nimitta	A sign; in meditation practice, a mental image which is usually visual.
Paṁsukūla	Discarded cloth; rag robes made of discarded cloth.
Paññā	Wisdom.
Parinibbāna	Final *Nibbāna* attained at the death of the Buddha or any of the *Arahants*.
Piṇḍapāta	Walking on the alms round to receive food.
Pūjā	Homage; devotion.
Rāga	Lust; sexual excitement; attachment.
Rūpa	Form; shape; the body.
Sākya	The race of people from whom the Buddha came.

Samādhi	Meditative calm; absorbed concentration, having many levels and types.
Samaṇa	A recluse; a practising Bhikkhu.
Saṁsāra	The total sphere of all the realms of existence.
Sangha	The order of Bhikkhus; a group of at least four Bhikkhus.
Sāsadā	The World Teacher; the Supreme Teacher; the Buddha as a teacher.
Sāsana	The Buddhist religion; the system of teaching and training taught by the Buddha.
Sati	Mindfulness.
Sāvaka	A hearer (of the teaching); usually those who heard the teaching directly from the Buddha.
Sīla	Morality; moral behaviour; the five moral precepts.
Ti-lakkhaṇa	The three characteristics of existence: impermanence, suffering and non-self.
Vassa	The annual 3-month rains retreat, when Bhikkhus are required to remain in a single residence.
Vaṭṭa	The continuing cycle of birth, life and death.

Inquiries may be addressed to:

Forest Dhamma Books
Baan Taad Forest Monastery
Udon Thani 41000
Thailand

fdbooks@gmail.com
www.forestdhammabooks.com